THINGS OF CONCERN

A Dissertation Relating To The State
Of The World And The State Of The Mind

By

Joseph K. Goldstein

—

Begun in 2001
Started long ago, but having grown in leaps
and bounds, just as any child should.

Written with concern,
That direction is unclear,
So what can we learn,
To protect our things so dear.
(What a lousy rhyme)

Order this book online at www.trafford.com
or email orders@trafford.com

Most Trafford titles are also available at major online book retailers.

Note for Librarians: A cataloguing record for this book is available from Library
and Archives Canada at www.collectionscanada.ca/amicus/index-e.html

Printed in Victoria, BC, Canada.

ISBN: 978-1-4269-1391-4 (sc)

ISBN: 978-1-4269-1392-1 (dj)

Library of Congress Control Number: 2009931994

*We at Trafford believe that it is the responsibility of us all, as both individuals and corporations,
to make choices that are environmentally and socially sound. You, in turn, are supporting this
responsible conduct each time you purchase a Trafford book, or make use of our publishing services.
To find out how you are helping, please visit www.trafford.com/responsiblepublishing.html*

*Our mission is to efficiently provide the world's finest, most comprehensive book publishing
service, enabling every author to experience success. To find out how to publish your book, your
way, and have it available worldwide, visit us online at www.trafford.com*

Trafford rev. 08/14/2009

Goldstein, Joseph K., 1938-
Things of Concern/ Joseph K. Goldstein .- 1ª ed. P. cm.

    1.   Sociology-21ª century-commentary

    2.   Politics-21ª century-commentary

 www.trafford.com

North America & international
toll-free: 1 888 232 4444 (USA & Canada)
phone: 250 383 6864 ♦ fax: 250 383 6804 ♦ email: info@trafford.com

The United Kingdom & Europe
phone: +44 (0)1865 487 395 ♦ local rate: 0845 230 9601
facsimile: +44 (0)1865 481 507 ♦ email: info.uk@trafford.com

DEDICATION
For my family-
To my wife Donna, and my two daughters Leah and Esther
Who I love so dearly,

and

For your family

and

as well, for everybody else

This page is a dedication to the confused. It acknowledges that we (the people) have a very messy life-process (being humanity), and rather interesting interpersonal/national/international relations, all based on the evolutionary fact that mankind is an amalgam of selfish, egotistical individuals; those egos having been developed to insure the survival of the individual in the face of multitudinous and varied lifetime interactions (with both people and things).

This of course, is because all of us are a consequence of formation through the ego development process: first the non-ego gets assaulted, and then ego-growth navigates away from any initial un-bias (one might argue, "as it should!!") through the many forms of imperfect interactions with the world. So the purity of new birth is immediately overpowered, and then the consequences are not even the ones expected; the consequence is "US", dressed as we are, in our "Sunday Best". It is no wonder so many of us are confused, we come from such different perspectives, and cannot agree that everyone, or anyone, else is right.

THINGS OF CONCERN

--Here's a Hearty List of Current and Potential Problems

--From this List, what common elements offer methods for resolution?

--Guess what, this list could be a table of contents for a book!!!!

The way the book is written, all subjects are covered, but maybe in a ranting methodology rather than an indexed coherence.

So read on and "enjoy?" because it has been my intense catharsis and satisfaction to write.

Preface-
By Way Of Saying How Do You Do

I write this book instigated by concerns regarding the tumultuous forces in play within the "Order of Man" as he exists in the world today. Many important events, and significantly, many important trends, have surfaced and are shaping the future of mankind. Some of the thoughts in this book are letters I have written, prepared under real-time extremes of concern with what is happening in the world. Shades of history show themselves. Contention amongst the various societies of current mankind are creating these extreme forces that, because of technological advance, have the potential to destroy all mankind, or to take the highest levels of societal existence and reduce it to the dark ages of 14th century existence once again.

I need to say a word (or two) about my thought processes: I am an avid proponent of the writings and ideas of Ayn Rand, and although anything I say is what I personally have developed, Ayn Rand and her contemporary, Andrew J. Galambos, have both significantly shaped my thoughts, my intellect, and even my emotional responses. Many of my ideas were developed subsequent to exposure to Mr. Galambos' lectures, as now released in his book Sic Itur Ad Astra. This all relates to the concept of action and reaction in that what we sow influences what we reap, and no matter what anyone says, the paths to a place are time-related and closed-loop, because as you move along and experience the "path- population" of either events, things, or people, you change and move a little bit differently than you might have when you initially entered the path. It's sort of like Roger Zelazny's "Amber" series, in that the protagonist and his immediate family have arguably either the ability to walk alternate universes or actually create alternate universes as they walk, and in which they act and live.

So look at the development of segmented mankind, and I do mean segmented, in that various societies have developed from physically isolated and culturally different backgrounds and therefore molded socially different people.   No one person can say with impunity that they themselves are right, because you have to believe that right is relative, unless you are omnipotent and absolute and know that everything you pass judgment on is a flawed version of your own ideal. And that means all of us. So the quandary is quite real that some of the realities just don't fit together. Rodney King said: "Can't we all just get along", and the Ayn Rand and Andrew J. Galambos answer that unless we all agree to a structure for society which is the same for all (local sub-corollaries allowed), where we all respect each others property, both physical and intellectual, we really can't "just get along".

We sort of used to, it sort of worked many years ago, before the globe became so much a community, when we were all physically separated, before technology put all of us easily within reach of each other and offered us force multipliers in terms of power levels and reach that we just never had before. At that time, society was the small world of your local environment.

We start life as a baby, as a little blank; emotionally, intellectually, spiritually, and interactively; ready for shaping acquired characteristics as molded by the environment and hereditary reaction; and hereditary characteristics, which are either fixed in their output, or allow and respond to external stimuli by creating reaction. All this comes down to the fact that one of the wonderful things about natural man is that he does change as he interacts with both his societal and physical world, and man still exists as a species. But again, what have evolved are several different world-views, and some of these have built-in inhibitors against working together. Hard not to make judgment unless you take one giant step up and say that everyone's goal is a stratagem for survival or else.   Now that's a heavy duty thought that should shake up any reader, but no way does it get everyone, because we have all been bred (through survival of the fittest) to know that you must take care of yourself first, and the problem is that we have been so shaped by our experiences and heredity that we pop out as a societal product, although admittedly, there are millions of versions of that product.

Some of the output is scary, because you can trace it back to some very hard-core drives, some that are mutually exclusive, and are part or cause of the problem facing mankind today. "How right must you be?", that is the question. And it leads to the next one, "to be or not to be? ". Now you have it, some societies have segments that absolutely know what is right and can't handle anything threatening them, and some just don't know that the road to self-destruction is not necessarily correct for all.

So with all that, as you can see from my table of contents, there are a lot of things that can and will be examined, and so we shall. But also note that this list does not include everything in the world, only the things that have caught my attention for the moment. I need to add, based on a strong input from one of my daughters, that what I am presenting in this book are opinions, and where important, I will back these opinions up with facts, but in general, what I have done is taken a situation and explored it intellectually, logically, and emotionally, and presented my considered output for your perusal.

You know....... each morning when I get to the computer, I look at a fresh bright screen with great Windows Wallpaper of Lakes at Mammoth, and I think WOW, what a wonderful start. Then I think about my subject material, and again, I think, what a good thing to be able to sit down, organize my thoughts, put them down on paper, and refine them into something I hope is coherent, interesting, and meaningful. That makes me happy, even though the material is sometimes a bit heavy and can weigh you down, yet I know it has merit. My writing is more than sporadic; it really is bites of my internal makeup. I don't care what the subject, because I have something to say about each and every subject, and many times, as I sit here, I surprise myself with how my fingers move so fast, form words and thoughts, and then when I read the material, I pull an "Urkle"- "did I do that?" I keep adding to this intro, because I feel that insight into my thought process is good for anyone that picks it up for a quick look.

Again, some of the following segments were real-time thoughts created during and immediately after the formative events. When I look at the content, I see that relevance still exists. And there is a common thread to the whole thing, it is more than a ranting and raving monologue, the thread is you, me, and <u>baby</u> makes three.

There is another thing that I noticed; as I am writing, I tend to write in spurts and additions (or changes to various sections), not chronologically, not in order, not even the same sections in sequence. Seems to be a sporadic excitement about a subject that spurs me into the mode and mood.

I have also split the presentation into two parts. The first, which is the main text, contains a lot of guttural aspects, it represents the thoughts that have congealed as a result of my concerns. The second part of the book is the addendum, which contains material intended to present resolution to the many diatribes of the first section.

I need to add that this book has been a while in the writing, over a period of many years, and with the addition of subject material and perspective as a function of this length of time. I worried for a while that the topics might lose relevance, but much to my chagrin, I see that man's nature and inclinations does not change much, and so everything remains current.

Additionally, as I developed the content and began formulating my concepts of solutions to the problems discussed, I came to realize that what is called "Volitional Science" represents a significant part of many of the solutions. Since I feel that the concepts of Volitional Science play such a major role in the solutions to so many of man's problems, I have consolidated parts of the theory into an appendix that will provide a first look for the interested reader. Since the Theory of Volition is so prevalently noted within this manuscript, it may also please the reader not only to review the appendix, but at some point refer to the book Sic Itur Ad Astra, Volume One, by Andrew J. Galambos, released April, 1999.

AND SO WE START:

Chapter 1 –Global Terrorism

This section spurred the creation of the whole document. It was the realization that the Free World is different as a result of the 9/11 affronts on humanity. Sure we all knew that there was always a fine line between order and chaos, and that all it takes is a very few to upset a balance. But now that the balance is upset, the Free World needs to gear up and contain the threat, and eliminate it in whatever way it can. Because progress can be forward or backward, depending on perspective, and darn it, I like to see progress as moving into the light, not the dark.

Open Letter On Global Terrorism
Part 1- "The Local Scene"

WE ARE THE SAME, ALL OF US. We care, and now we fear. It is not cowardice, but instead the awareness that purity in our lives is under attack by these acts of terrorism. I NEED to take action, and know that we are the same, that you too feel the threat, and want to act. So I have started by putting some thoughts together. I am sending them to you, in the hopes that they strike a similar vibration, and begin a really important initiative towards the elimination of terrorist activity. For all of us-our kids, neighbors, our future as humanity, ourselves. I really want the right thoughts and acts to surface a safe world for us all.

To our future,

Joe Goldstein

A Patriotic Effort: May 22, 2002

Let me introduce myself. I am just an American- a guy with a wife, and two kids in college, and recently retired from the work force after 41 years of engineering in aerospace. And now my world is turned upside down, just the same as everyone else's. I know that terrorist attacks on the United States and Western culture have been carefully orchestrated through small cells and independent plans, established within and against the freedoms of this society. They are time bombs moving inexorably to release. I am not happy, because I want to contribute something to eliminate these terrible possibilities, but right now, I am not sure what that should be.

I see our military response to these attacks, and am recognizing that pure force alone will not provide resolution. I am not privy to the more cloistered of diplomatic and military activity, but I see a parallel to conditions in the State of Israel, where the forces of destruction are willing to die with the promise of martyrdom. But I do not wish to address this death wish, merely to pre-empt the ability of such forces to complete their destructive deeds.

As of this moment, I don't yet see the direct path to how my energies, as a civilian, as a threatened citizen, can be harnessed productively in a way to aid my country. Somehow I know that each and every American and each and every person/creed/nation that values innocent life, can come together to overcome these efforts of destruction. A world coalition of people will support the political coalitions sought by governments in the effort to establish a world free from terrorism.

Starting at a grass-roots level, I see that development of a neighborhood mind-set would start a really positive process. I absolutely do not foster any citizen vigilante approach because that would over-ride the basic freedoms upon which our societies have been based. It would damage the innocent and create havoc. Rather, I support the establishment of local groups, focused on preservation of our freedoms. To prevent excesses in the name of freedom, these groups must represent a positive movement, not as citizen police, but rather in a close "neighborhood-watch" relation that embraces all neighborhoods and residents. Whether in a tenement, condominium, townhouse, apartment, farm, private dwelling neighborhood-this concept supports a personal familiarity that instantaneously provides local happenings, information, events, people movement, etc...

I believe an expansion and redirection of the current "neighborhood watch" concept, originally formed to thwart local crime, can have an infrastructure which can be expanded to a higher, loftier, and more urgent goal. Changes would be required, such as charter and purpose, which would be established by and at a national level. This would include patriotic awareness, neighborhood awareness, and clear limits to activity and authority of the group. I know that current address databases offer logical areas of influence. What would be important is a tie-in with authority to empower the local chapters to work within very stringent but meaningful constraints, and to foster two-way communication from the local group to police, the city, the state, and the federal government.

This sounds like a big bite, but frankly, America and the Free World needs to use and empower its citizenry and imbed a methodology for the protection of our freedoms, one without unnecessary financial burden further eroding our standards of living. This is a voluntary approach that I can support. I am a person who needs to contribute, wants to contribute; and I am afraid that without all of us helping, we will be the weaker for it.

Most importantly, if we put this structure and organization in place now, it will be tried, tested, ready, and operating before and hopefully obviating, any future events. It needs to be now, we cannot keep waiting until the next one and the next one and the next one. We cannot be a paper tiger with ineffectual response.

Please think about this. I send this to my friends-pass it on for others to review and improve. I send this to my congressman and other political figures in the hopes that all will embrace this patriotic calling. If it seems appropriate, then legislation could be immediately introduced to create and support "National Watch". I call on all of you who read this to forward it to others and vocalize support to your congressmen. I rely on the congressional personnel to whom this is sent to acknowledge constituent support as it comes in, and to implement this program.

In sincerity,

J. K. Goldstein

AN ADJUNCT TO THE LETTER
part 2- "going beyond local"

WE ARE THE SAME, ALL OF US. We care, and now we fear. It is not cowardice, but instead the awareness that purity in our lives is under attack by these acts of terrorism. I NEED to take action, and know that we are the same, that you too feel the threat, and want to act. So I have started by putting some thoughts together. I am sending them to you, in the hopes that they strike a similar vibration, and begin a really important initiative towards the elimination of terrorist activity. For all of us-our kids, our neighbors, and future humanity- I really want the right thoughts and acts to surface a safe world for us all.

To our future,

Joe Goldstein

A Position on Terrorism: May 23, 2002

First, let me once again introduce myself. I am just an American- a guy with a wife, and two kids in college, and recently retired from the work force after 41 years of engineering in aerospace. And now my world is turned upside down, just the same as everyone else's. After a lot of agonizing during the past few weeks, I have written this message as an addition to my initial reactions to the terrorist activities.

The complex issue of fighting terrorism must consider containment, elimination, restitution, and at the very worst- retribution. Immediate focus must be on the perpetrating terrorists. A second focus must be placed on those who aid and abet these individuals. Thirdly, but by no means last, is a focus on the organizations that sponsor and support such acts- not the terrorist cell, but the root source. Such people and their organizations must be totally and permanently defused.

Multi-pronged response to terrorism necessitates addressing both the urgent and the important fronts. <u>Most urgent</u> are actions necessary to thwart incipient acts, requiring that the actual terrorist cells be located. No safe harbor, no working environment, can be allowed. Into whichever country they enter, they endanger every citizen, because neither ethnic nor religious origin reduces the threat of biological or nuclear impact to a citizen in a country under terrorist attack. In fact, the danger increases with proximity if the perpetrators seek anonymity within such a community.

Although anti-terrorist response is the jurisdiction of special government agencies such as the FBI, CIA, DHS, and International Police, they are all supported by local law enforcement and local community activity. To foster efficient, complete, and devastating enforcement, authority is provided to these entities, allowing anti-terrorist agencies the capability to pre-empt these actions. Communities need to form and support citizen "Neighborhood Watch"/ "National Watch", promoting an expanded charter which recognizes the dire situation existing today. These watch groups would have as a mission the fostering of patriotic awareness, neighborhood awareness, and a familiarity with the residents and transients of each neighborhood. The groups would operate under very clear limits of activity established on a national level, to insure that they do not exceed lawful authority. Timely and relevant information obtained by the group would be presented to authority as soon as uncovered.

The second part of this approach involves additional personnel availability for involvement in anti-terrorist activity. The population of this country includes a large percentage of retired people who are enjoying the benefits resulting from many years of hard work, and who also wish to pass this legacy on to their progeny. I am one of these people. I am no longer part of the work force, and this is by choice. However, also by choice, I want and need to be a part of this effort to overcome threats to my way of life. So in addition to every citizen doing their part, perhaps retirees can be tapped for time and expertise in special ways of fighting terrorism.

The third portion of this approach involves the global community. As an underlying premise, root cause of these terrorist acts is their own perception of threat and therefore a cultivated and developed hatred against the West. The issue lies in the desire of the Muslim Fundamentalists to remain pure and cloistered from other venues. Their ways are threatened by the global nature of technology today, including free trade, communication, transportation, personal interaction, and perceptions of human rights. Going beyond an embargo based on retribution, this situation can logically be turned in the right direction. Political action can and should involve supporting both terrorist and anti-terrorist goals of total isolation of such terrorist mind-set from global interaction. This means focus on those governments who sponsor, aid, and abet such activity.

Response must be on an international level. Here the international community, through the United Nations, is a perfect forum. Paraphrasing U. S. President George W. Bush, "there are only two possible positions on terrorism; either you are against the terrorists or an enemy of those against the terrorists". Grey does not exist- there is no neutral position, and there can be no dealings of appeasement through fear, because that is the method of terrorism. The steps in the establishment of positions are already in motion through diplomatic coalition. National leadership in each and every country of the world must take a position of condemnation, or else they will be condoning terrorist acts. This schism falls within the charter of the United Nations, with a clear and absolute position to expel any nation that condones and supports terrorist activity to achieve global ends. United Nations action must take the form of embargo and isolation.

Make no mistake; these words and such actions create a terrible scenario. For all the years of human history, there have always been wars, always have and have-nots, always aggressors and victims. Finally, in this age of technology and world-level communication and activity, humanity has the opportunity to overcome these issues. But that is not yet today's world situation, mainly because education towards understanding and appreciation of these issues relates to individual environment. Insular conditions that oppose unbiased, untainted thinking exist in many areas of the world. Many atrocious conditions are accepted as normal by such societies. Blatant shortfalls as measured against some societies are not at issue in others. The people involved, not outside observers, establish judgment. Until such time as people themselves feel the need for change, we can see the consequence of, and response to, humanitarian attempts to influence these areas- its name is Terrorism. It is the dastardly last strike-back resort of insularity.

On a global level then, perhaps the right solution is to once again establish a "cold war" mentality, this time identifying the forces of terrorism as the cancer they are, and to insure an isolationist situation for any nation supporting terrorism, forcing it into its own private and secular existence. Such a nation would NOT benefit from the advances of, and interactions with, free society. The world community would shun such a nation and its representatives. However, the free world would always embrace those who would wish to leave such insular existence, and provide choice to those who would enter a free world environment through the concept of ASYLUM.

Accomplishing those major goals will not be easy, especially since isolation of nations of terror requires strong moral and ethical commitment by those opposed to terrorism. Mankind may not be ready to band together as one, in pursuit of moral and intellectual correctness. To this point in time, the world's nations have developed as geographical and geo-political entities, with major interaction based on the self-interests of trade, profit, and self-protection.

The worst aspect of this approach is the possible "coalition of the banned". This must be addressed. Perhaps it is time for a third concept, for the giant leap of mankind towards the concepts of "Volitional Science", a concept of bringing thinking minds and intellects to a higher goal, that of respect for the individual and his property. We must respect each other, for we will exist or perish based on our ways of dealing with each other. We have moved so far forward in both physical and biological science that we have created the ability to destroy ourselves. Terrorists with fanatical elements rewarded in and after death cannot be dealt with as reasoning entities in this world. World sponsored education promoting respect for property, both physical and intellectual, becomes the necessary cornerstone to the creation of an enduring free world civilization.

Through education, through free choice, and given the time to achieve, mankind will develop right relations between people and nations.

Please think about this. I send this to my friends- to pass on for others to review and improve. I send this to my congressman and other political figures in the hopes that all will embrace this patriotic calling. If it seems appropriate, then legislation could be immediately introduced to create and support these initiatives. I call on all of you who read this to forward it to others and vocalize support to your congressman. I rely on the congressional personnel to whom this is sent to acknowledge constituent support as it comes in, and to foster and implement this program.

In sincerity,

J. K. Goldstein

ANOTHER ADJUNCT TO THE LETTER
part 3-"who are you?"

WE ARE THE SAME, ALL OF US. We care, and now we fear. It is not cowardice, but instead the awareness that purity in our lives is under attack by these acts of terrorism. I NEED to take action, and know that we are the same, that you too feel the threat, and want to act. So I have started by putting some thoughts together. I am sending them to you, in the hopes that they strike a similar vibration, and begin a really important initiative towards the elimination of terrorist activity. For all of us-our kids, our neighbors, and future humanity- I really want the right thoughts and acts to surface a safe world for us all.

To our future,

Joe Goldstein

Steps in the Right Direction: May 24, 2002

First, let me once again introduce myself. I am just an American- a guy with a wife, and two kids in college, and recently retired from the work force after 41 years of engineering in aerospace. And now my world is turned upside down, just the same as everyone else's. After a lot of agonizing during the past few weeks, I have added even more to my initial reactions to the terrorist activities.

Drastic events require drastic action. The events: the World Trade Center attack, biological anthrax, and future unknown threats, such as to bridges, stadiums, museums, major buildings, cities, reservoirs, public transportation. The action- a change in the mind-set of the free world, and the institution of a security structure within our society. The free world, which has been forging ahead towards an affluent efficiency fostered by free enterprise, must revamp societal actions to add the non-productive layers of a security system to insure the survival of the human race.

Some top-level thoughts are presented as general observation, and can act as catalysts for further detailed planning.

Citizen groups formed for the purpose of protection represent an extremely positive move. They essentially create a universal support group work force with a proprietary interest in doing well. Care must be taken to insure that the group will not become overzealous. National charter and purpose is essential as a set of strict guidelines to bound activity.

I CANNOT OVER-EMPHASIZE THIS. Be aware that every free country is in imminent danger. The training and departure of terrorists from their original camps has been completed, and now there are possible sleeper cells in every free country. Using illegal papers such as forged passports and driver's licenses, and the laxity of border control in some countries, such people can and have entered and assimilated. But note, although low profile, no person actually exists in total isolation. Needs, such as food and equipment, forces these individuals to venture into the community at some level. Within the community, truly suspicious actions could be observed and described to suitable authority. Such actions cannot be ignored. NO ONE in society is immune to the dangers posed by these people. No community is risk free. It is essential that this be clearly recognized, by all people, from the local neighborhood to the sovereign state. NO ONE is risk free. At worst, if such terrorist actions continue, then retribution in kind might be the result, and escalation would only be a matter of time. NO ONE and NO PLACE is risk free.

At a higher level, the illegal alien coupled with terrorist mentality must be identified, isolated, and removed. Sovereign nations have that responsibility to their citizens. Checking interim and expired visas is definitely a forward step. Then, as an additional method of action, a bar code identification card and a verifying lie detector program could be put in place. Each and every person would be required to have such a card, which would then be entered into a database file. This card becomes valid only after the individual has taken and passed the lie detector test. I read and concur with a descriptor for this card, in an article in 10/29/01 Aviation Week, in which the smart card could contain retinal scan, face and voice recognition, hand geometry, and fingerprints. This card would require concurrency with taking a lie detector test. The test questions would be ordered to properly categorize terrorist propensity or actuality. Once again, national guidelines would be essential to insure that the bounds of privacy are respected and that the questions are relevant only to the issues.

This program would offer a grace period for the initial card and test, to allow an orderly transition. All individuals will require this card in order to conduct any form of transaction, as well as being subject to roving spot checks, and those without cards after the grace period required to immediately obtain one. The test would also be administered periodically for those who have cards.

Thus, this method offers three safeguards to insure a non-terrorist citizenry. First, having the card with adequate identifiers contained on it to insure that the holder is per the descriptor. Second, having a national database, against which the card is immediately checked, to insure card validity and validating that the test was satisfactorily completed. This insures that the card is not bogus. And third, that roving spot checks with an adequate portable card reader/check system, linked back to the national database, will both insure that a person has a valid card, or that a person must get the test and card immediately. The card readers can be suitably encrypted to insure against card or information falsification.

(Addition, 9/05-There needs to be much more thought given to this than is currently written above, because care must be taken to prevent an escalation into national hysteria and a police-like state.)

At a higher level: the United Nations is a perfect organization to act as the Voice of Humanity. The clear threat of Weapons of Mass Destruction is to the human race, not to a power group, not to a special interest group, not to a religious or social group, not to a nation. There is no doubt that response in kind is possible, but clear heads need to insure that such does not happen. Escalation of such dire weaponry will produce chaos and destruction that can end only in obliteration. It is essential that the United Nations actively support this program. It is essential that the U.N. military arm, consisting of personnel from each and every member country, who must have U. N. allegiance first, and national allegiance subservient during their time of service, be charged with this duty. Any country not in support of the destruction of terrorism will be barred from world political involvement. There can be no alternative- this is not an issue of differences, but issue of survival.

Please think about this. I send this to my friends- to pass on for others to review and improve. I send this to my congressman and other political figures in the hopes that all will embrace this patriotic calling. If it seems appropriate, then legislation could be immediately introduced to support the initiatives. I call on all of you who read this to forward it to others and vocalize support to your congressman. I rely on the congressional personnel to whom this is sent to acknowledge constituent support as it comes in, and to foster and implement this program.

In sincerity,

J. K. Goldstein

TODAY, July 7, 2005 AND WHAT IT MEANS
part 4 -"and it doesn't stop"

Today, in London, 4 bombs exploded in four different sections of London. They killed over 30, injured over 1000 -everyone just a regular person, going about his or her daily life. This needs to be thought through, because immediate reactive action may not be the thing to do.

First: a discussion of motive and intent.

Part of the news release claiming responsibility (which by the way is a heinous thing to be proud of) states that England is a Zionist Crusading nation and was involved in both Afghanistan and Iraq. So the terrorist rationalization is that England is a Judeo-Christian sympathizer and that any involvement with Muslim activity or States is a cause of fault. Starting at the beginning, remember that 9/11 was a first strike by the terrorists, and that the Iraq situation, no matter its start, is now a political situation, which is hopefully in process of resolution involving the religious representation, and will be played out by the Iraqis themselves. The Afghanistan invasion was a clear response to the Taliban government stated support for the terrorists that caused 9/11. And the Judeo-Christian ethic is a non-threat to anyone, not a single goal is directed against others.

So what we have is a clear desire to foment a fear, and hatred by the West, of Islamic followers, with the intent of polarizing everyone into a chaotic situation. There is no doubt that Western civilization cannot take the position that Spain took, of abdicating moral and political responsibility to (in the short-term) safeguard its own future and its citizens. Bowing to terrorist demands only creates more demands, and since there is no government with which to deal, is clearly a ploy to continue terrorist action.

A non-win situation is created, but perhaps a solution can surface. This goes into the condition of isolation. I talked about this before, with the thought that perhaps a solution that closes "Terrorist Borders" and guarantees their insularism, while offering a porous way out through professed desire to embrace Western political ideology, would be a possibility.

This is some very serious stuff, from three perspectives. Most people, and I mean the one's in "target" countries, think that what is happening has a low probability of affecting them. So the thinking is convoluted in the thought that "I" am not involved, and the people "I" know are not involved, and that the chances that this will happen to anyone within "my" sphere is infinitesimal. This is erroneous thinking, because although probability works against it, surely it can happen to you or me.

Secondly, jump beyond the ego, and look in terms of what a terrorist act represents. It is two-fold in itself; a blunt flaunting of what freedom is all about, and a direct challenge to your way of life. Here we are, in a country where you can be anything, do anything, make a future for yourself, choose your belief system, your friends, your very way of life, and now comes a very large threat which has the consequence of obviating all the things that your life had become. Travel at risk, be questioned to insure safety, reduce global economy and reduce affluence, just a few. Your very existence is threatened. The development of decades of diplomacy allowing interaction between countries, reducing border limitations, allowing a monetary flow and interchange, extensive commerce, sharing of resources, and the raising of the overall poverty level as the result of commercial interaction, sharing of health research results. What is not affected?

And third, the impact on the people identified with, associated with, or in proximity of the terrorists. This one is a tougher call, because many who are not radical have already expressed preference by leaving the radical area. But the majority is within the countries in question, and many are unable to do more than live within the means available. Many would be happy to stay where they are (status quo), this the result of up-bringing and form of education. I would tend to think that 75% of the people would accept whatever form of government is imposed, so long as they can survive. Something like 10% represent the radical thinking of extremism, and the other 15% support it. Don't know how right these statistics are, but they could represent a reason why democracy is attacked. If more than 50% support democracy, then the others cannot dare allow free choice. Instead, what is offered is the way of the fist, which totally represses the idea of free and thoughtful selection.

AN ADJUNCT TO July 7 –
part 5-"round-up time"

Well, I've been thinking even more and more about this, and it is pretty straightforward.

Ben Ladin and extremist Muslims have initiated this terrorism campaign with several goals in mind. The biggest and most universal seems to be the total isolation of the Muslim world from the Western world. This is not hard to attempt, the concept of violence and "backwash-fear" promote Western distrust of anything Muslim, while the rhetoric and any Western reaction tend to polarize some of the Muslim community. If this progresses it could eventually lead to accomplishment of that secular goal. Why would this be done? It could be fear and loathing of all things Western. Fear because Western values and Western ways may very well be appealing. They may also be introducing the possibility of bringing the population out of the time-honored ages of the past, and be introducing the possibilities of a worldwide community. Loathing, because the upbringing of many has included the propaganda of hatred, the propaganda similar to that of the Nazi regime, a selection of enemies upon whom to direct passionate emotions of hate. It includes the twisting of holy works and thoughts, and the creation of such deep conviction that life itself is secondary to a(n) (false) ideal.

So there are basically three types of Muslim peoples involved: westernized and accepting and practicing Western values (whether living in the West or not), those who to this point have not selected sides and want nothing more than to live their lives and to some degree are willing to follow a good path to betterment, and those who are radicalized and want to foment acrimony and eventual separation of Western values from Muslim life. Well, to look into the future, I agree with an article I read today in the Daily News by Thomas Friedman, he suggested that unless the terrorist faction is stopped, a great divide is in the offing. Stopping the terrorist faction needs to come from within the Muslim community, the community needs to clearly condemn the terrorist faction. This because the terrorist ways threaten the Muslim community, the world community, and humanity. We cannot have a dark and unaccountable group continuously wrecking havoc on the civilized world. It must stop. It is a cancer to civilization. And "It" has two solutions. One is elimination, the other is isolation. I have talked about isolation, somewhat of a great wall, which keeps the two factions apart. This is a terrible blow to the concept of a world community, which due to technological advances in travel and communication, is on a threshold of blossoming into a wonderful era of humankind. The trouble is that suitably constructed and solidly based education is necessary to provide the scruples, the framework, and the basis for peaceful co-existence of all peoples.

Chapter 2- "WMD"-Thoughts On Polarization- March, 2004

My thoughts have been reeling with world terrorism. Things are polarizing in the worst way for the world, not the best way, even for the terrorist mind.

The escalating events of 9/11, suicide bombings and the reprisals, fighting in Afghanistan, Islamic sentiment, threats involving Iraq, threats of Al-Queda retaliation, strong U. S. position, weak ally resolve, and a growing strength of Arab unity- all point to a dangerous direction for world events.

Of course, as usual, everyone's perspective seems right to him, whether ruled by logic, emotion, faith, fear, or hatred. Everyone thinks they are right based on their beliefs, agendas, and goals. That is always the hardcore cause of conflict-laden situations. Now these situations apply to the world, because even cursory examination shows that technology has placed us in a global, not a regional arena.

Consider- the large, well infra-structured U.S. is forced to divert a large portion of Gross National Product affluence to the establishment of safeguards against terrorism. Israel lives with an overwhelming amount of security yet almost daily deaths. Many civilized nations, concerned about their own citizens, are expending effort to create anti-terrorism controls, but are distancing themselves from embracing this as a major conflict, on the false assumption that terrorist initiatives are not aimed specifically at them. The Arab nations that are placing their ethnic support with terrorist groups have regressed from their emergence into a world-view back to a secular one, and have pushed themselves back 1000 years in the process. This, at a time when there are global consequences to any action.

It is terrible to realize that the force of destruction available to nations and factions is the very deterrent force of the zero-sum game created by major powers to insure that they never be used. This activity was the naïve product of 20th century nationalistic political and military minds. Now holders of these fearsome WMD's threaten to place the world hostage. There is no thought to the consequences to humankind.

Not surprisingly, I have a personal position on this subject, but I have to say that <u>anything</u> that polarizes opinion will, by its very nature, contribute to and inflame the current tense situation. Because, though we speak of global conditions, we do not have a globally based method to deal with such situations. Individuals, groups, and nations all have their own agendas and do not want to agree to a common good. Even the United Nations cannot deal with a global threat, in that "peace-keeping" is totally limited by the concurrence requirements of nationalistic interests.

Many alternative solutions are being proposed; but they are focused on de-fusing rather than resolving. It is time that the civilized world recognizes that an over-riding body MUST be formed to address the danger of human annihilation, a body capable of responding with both world-view perspective and force, if required. This group will differ from the U.N. in that it will <u>not</u> deal with day-to-day international issues. This body will consist of plenipotentiary representation from all nations, dedicated to insuring a world future. It will have a military support branch to insure that declarations are acknowledged.

Five major steps must be implemented. The first is the drafting of a charter for the group, which must focus on world/global threats. The second is creating the agenda for acting on the issues at hand, namely: "The Potential of World Terrorism to Create World Instability Leading to Use of WMD and "The Potential that WMD will Annihilate the Human Race". The third step is to address all causes of these situations. The fourth is the considerations of resolution and redress. (Care must be taken to prevent retribution as a goal, since strong display of "get-even" force would only foment conflict.) The fifth step is action.

The tools necessary to resolve the issues are anchored in the logic, emotion, faith, fear, and hatred that initiated the conflicts. Each of these elements must be understood, and satisfactorily addressed. That means that in recognition of the powerful propaganda which initiated the emotional components, a suitable salve must be found. That means that in spite of what might seem irrefutable logic and good sense, such might not address imagined grievances. BE ASSURED, PERCEPTION IS THE KEY: NOT LOGIC, NOT EVEN TRUTH.

So what to do? It starts with a campaign to propagate this message, and to initiate an overwhelming ground swell showing that people are worried about their futures, the future of their children, the survival of all we hold dear, and the very world upon which we live. We must reach out globally, because only when everyone is of one mind can we feel safe that the threat to life as we know it is removed. It must start now, because too many minds and emotions want to wreck havoc and destruction, and to start potentially non-stoppable, escalating, and devastating action.

I send this to my friends-see its message and talk with others. I send this to my congressman and other political figures-embrace this as your own, for certainly it is, and start action towards implementation. This is no longer watching your back, it is now watching the sky; and the world cannot afford to see anything dangerous up there.

Thank you,

Joe Goldstein

WMD

Are we big boys, or what? I think not, because the toys we have created are more dangerous than just to us. Remember when you were a little kid, and everybody tried so hard to sensitize you to every little bit of danger? "Don't go too fast, watch out for the slope, don't cut your finger, and don't fall off the tree." Did we listen? Maybe to some things, but being the adventurous tykes that we were, we did a lot of things anyway, and we ran home crying after some of the predictions came true.

Well, we graduate into bigger things and bigger consequences. So you have to think about what mentalities can do the research, the development, and the production of some of our brainchildren. We don't have to start with WMD, because that is simply the culmination, we can look at almost anything we have created and developed, and see the same potentials lurking or existing in them.

Let's start with the little baby, each and every one an impressionable little being, and at that early point, maybe containing propensities, but certainly not ardent desires. It's our molding process that creates the arrowheads; it's our environments that create our reactive methods. And as we grow and get reinforced, we learn to apply our reactive capabilities to all the things we do. So the problems start with environment as it influences our genetic propensities. Translated, that means our parents, our friends, our neighborhoods. What's missing? Some will certainly say nothing is missing. But I think that is not true. Balance is essential, not polarization. Although becoming an expert is a lauded goal, there are building blocks that should be in place to carefully build the pyramid toward specialization. Don't like to see a leaning over into any one direction without seeing a balancing anchor.

Man is the only creature that molds his environment, the only creature that thinks, dreams, and then can act on those dreams. That is the one thing that differentiates man from other animals. Man makes changes in nature to suit his needs. I say "that is good". I am proud of mankind being able to lift up from animal status to civilization. But, we haven't really moved in balance with the surroundings, our internal mechanisms are still not fully coordinated. I keep heading towards what is termed "Volitional Science", but boy, is that ever a major factor or lack thereof in man's development.

You know what, I don't really need to talk much about WMD, because that threat is so big, that we all know enough about it. We have to support the people who are trying to rein in the blatant misuse of the elements that allow such creation and have created WMD, but we need to get back to source and correction. Diplomatic negotiations are a definite right step for handling some of the proliferation. It cannot be blackmail on the part of the holder of WMD; it needs to be a two-phase program. First the tentative exploration of disarming, and if that is ineffective, then overwhelming corrective action is required. This needs to be clearly stated in policy; so that there is no doubt that the world will be behind the actions to be taken. No threat of use of WMD can be tolerated, no threat condoned, and the consequences of its use must absolutely be absolute. Nothing redundant there, just plain in-your-face response that has no ifs, ands, or buts, about it.

Let's keep going on this. Research is the key for humanity moving ahead. It is the frontrunner after the start of thinking. It cannot be curtailed, much as that might curtail some of the twisted applications of the research. Rather, there needs to be purity and direction in what the energy devoted to research will produce.

Thinking about WMD does not require that it be broken into categories of destructive capability- the word MASS covers it. However, to the scientific and military mind this is insufficient, because that mind cannot deal with abstracts. On the political plane, it is easier to see the cover umbrella of WMD, but when it comes to countering it physically, the details are essential. So we see two approaches to dealing with the subject, and probably many possible approaches in dealing with the purveyors. Can we handle this politically? I think yes to a majority of the issue, but here is where the darn military mindset is essential. Because when you look at Nuclear, it is different than biological or chemical. Nuclear needs the sophisticated manufacturing techniques to produce the dangerous product.

Step back first. We are in a time-framed situation where the elements are available to produce the awful product. It can be any of the three (chemical, biological, or nuclear), because all are within the technological capabilities of today's man. So no argument about that. The next view is of the ability to produce, and then the last is the ability to disseminate. That is what needs to be assailed, because the threat to the perpetrator does no good, the terrorist mind has no problem in annihilation of others or of self. Countering the terrorist ability is the only possible answer at this time. That means cutting off the knowledge, the tools, the equipment, and the resources to produce a product. That means identifying the individuals, or an ability to locate the product, and then to eliminate them both. It will take dedication as well as information. Location is key; the people and the places need to be identified. Again, two methods. One is to access accomplices; the second is use technology to ferret out the assemblage and dissemination points. People are a key to this. The secretive nature of terrorist planning and the sharing only with select equally fanatic individuals creates a major challenge. Part of the solution lies in ideology. The challenge is to sever the zealousness of the fanatic, to clearly show individuals the alternate paths. This will not be easy to take a brainwashed or indoctrinated mind and back pedal to achieve a fair balance. It does not matter how that is done. It is a necessary arm of survival to do it. The second method, the locating through technology, is just as important in that it creates alternative solutions, because the first is a long uphill intellectual and emotional road, while the technology approach is an equally long research road. They need to be in place, they need to be happening. When you think about time-line, they must run ahead of the production and dissemination process.

I remember when the big issue was the "Atomic or Hydrogen" bomb, and how everyone was sooo freaky about its affect on the minds of the adults, as well as the young- how the concept of such raw power was supposedly warping the minds of youth. Frankly, I think it did to some extent. And now we have its equivalent in the terrorist, because such people can and will offer the same destruction. We need to move out and move on.

Joseph K. Goldstein

Some Thoughts On The U.S. Quandry-March 2004

The upcoming election will surely have the situation in Iraq as a big issue. Was it right going in, did we understand what we were getting into; should we still be there? These are all good questions, and needful of answers, because we are in an extremely precarious situation.

There are many perspectives to consider, but one stands out as the most pivotal. That is that the terrorism being conducted is a consequence of a very long-range plan. The schools that taught and trained young Islamic children to be faith-full killers and suicide terrorists have been in existence for at least 25 years, with a history that goes back thousands of years. The hatred of the West and Western society has been cultivated all these years, with the goal of countering the spread of democracy, the spread of free enterprise, the spread of any cultural perspective other than that of the extremist Muslim view. Further, it is known that the suicide culprits responsible for the 9/11 disaster planned and trained for the crashes starting at least 2 years earlier. Once again, evidence of a far-reaching plan to bring hatred, death, and chaos to the West.

Western reaction to suicide terrorists has been extremely difficult to properly implement. This is because there is no state or country to condemn; it is groups of people who are the perpetrators. Obtaining sufficient information to bound these situations is difficult, especially since terrorist organizations are working as cells, widely spread throughout the Eastern and Western world.

The United States, through the Bush administration, has implemented a response plan based on the generalization that although all the culprits cannot be identified, that some selected examples of retribution serve as indicator that the free world cannot accept the threat and actions of terrorism.

An Open Letter To My Leadership

April 26, 2004

The White House

Washington, D.C.

Dear President Bush and Staff:

I have concerns about the world situation, as I am sure you do as well. I have concerns about my country taking on responsibilities beyond the charter of a world participant in democracy. However, one of the differences between us is that you have a more direct hand and input into creating such conditions- that is why I am writing this letter.

As with us all, my thoughts and actions relate to the things of importance in my life; and my decisions are the result of the experiences I have had, methods I have been taught, and beliefs I have embraced. I am a retired Aerospace System Engineer, familiar with the concepts of requirements, trade-off studies, utility theory, and the various tools of decision-making. I typically premise that there are an extremely complex set of conditions versus alternatives upon which a person (and his advisors) would base decisions and choices for action. To the point, my first criteria when considering my world is that I am firm in insuring the safety of my family, and my country. So clearly, I ardently concur that safeguards are required to prevent terrorist activity from impacting my future. I also have a second criterion that helps govern my actions. This relates to validating the conditions for any form of action, just to be sure I will not be initiating anything I would subsequently regret.

Always, there is the ubiquitous "do-nothing" and the "do-everything" solutions as the two extremes of any decision matrix. Those and the in-between alternatives are solutions that must logically connect to the input conditions. It is the input conditions that distress me, because in addition to military and terrorist threat, there exists the considerable weight of world public opinion. There must be acknowledgement of the results of action and how to live with them. Here is the crux of my concern-the Azores Summit consisted of four world powers- the US, Britain, Portugal, and Spain. Yes, many of the other nations of the world may have privately supported these four, but were concerned that a strong and aggressive position could not assure that future threats would be eliminated. Many of these countries have ethnic, religious, or social considerations that do not offer them clear-cut solutions to this problem. Therefore, world problems require that social order be an important parameter.

I know that government decision-makers have large research and support staffs to insure examining all considerations, and that many more facts and presumptions concerning threats and counters are reviewed than become available to the average citizen. These balance against the international and domestic view of our policies, as well as the real time consequences of our potential actions and their follow-on effects. In the big picture, although immediate needs demand immediate action (with decisions made so that long term results would be world beneficial), the intermediate result (such as international isolation, pre-emptive strike as a national policy against sovereign nations, reprisal by the remaining small groups of vicious-weapon-equipped madmen, and an economy burdened by supporting large conflicts), is that we put ourselves into a very narrow box. It places the nation and its citizens out on a limb of public and political fervor, which is an open threat heading to possible disaster.

The proper use of such decision matrices and briefings will result in best usage of the separation and balance of powers within the government, fostering a biased, but actually quite fair, play to all the necessary players.
Because of this, I would dearly like more insight into the factors that make our national decisions. These decisions and policies affect me, my family, my neighborhood, my way of life, and my life. I recognize that a portion of such data may well be classified in the public interest, and not available to the general populace, but yet; cleaning up the presentation of these aspects, the information could be formulated into a decision matrix that can be provided to everyday citizens. Your voting citizenship consists of thinking, concerned people, all affected by and a part of the world-whole. This citizenship elected you, and allowed

appointment of many of your staff. In that respect, you are me, and when it comes to life-threatening times, I want to understand.

Please gear government press briefings and releases towards providing more complete information, allowing the citizen reader/listener to truly feel comfortable with the decisions of his government.

For example, I have tried to step back, with the knowledge I have received though the media, to see if there is any obvious positive program that can surface to accomplish what I consider the most important of goals- safety and well being of my family, and by extension- the country and the world. I start with exactly where we are today-bogged down in the warlike actions and threats associated with terrorist and aggressive response activities.

I believe that we need to gain international support in eliminating terrorism as a way of action and as a threat-and that way is to establish a really world-oriented policy. I believe that world orientation means world participation. I believe that we must consider a change that puts international teeth into the United Nations. The single overlying requirement of the entire UN body should be to insure that no threat disturbs peace anywhere in the world. All other function, although real, would be secondary. That does not mean stopping current activities; it means priority to a <u>Prime Requirement</u>. Implementation of this charter would start with peaceful monitoring, and if cause were identified, it would elicit punitive consequences if not resolved through immediate negotiations, which would not be allowed to exceed a specified time limit. This simple enactment and empowerment would be through the creation of a properly equipped international peacekeeping force with the charter to support the UN Prime Requirement. This force would be populated with personnel who would embrace allegiance to a world body, not a nation.

This must be proposed now, as an alternative to the localized actions in Iraq, Afghanistan, North Korea, Israel, and who knows where next. Through such a U.S. proposal, we create a graceful withdrawal method from our current confrontations, and form an internationally acceptable compromise, which all nations must support.

Please, I repeat, please, let this thought ferment, and let it grow to maturity. Our country, our people, our world, cannot sustain the current confrontations without terribly dire consequences.

Thank you,
Joseph K. Goldstein

Chapter 3-Global Conflict

Once upon a time, the term global conflict referred to a "World War", notice the capitalization. All of a sudden, things have changed and the concept of global is much broader. Well, that's probably a better way to view it. It involves enough entities that the danger of involving everyone is incipient.

Once it could have meant fighting together (maybe against disease, or poverty). That might even make sense, but that wouldn't really scare anyone, it might merely mobilize them. Now, with the threat of death anywhere and everywhere, the ostrich nations have elected not to see it coming or happening. Well, mobilization is essential to prevent the current state of skirmish (I know, thousands of dead are hardly a skirmish), but the escalating consequences are the scariest part of all. Because soon enough if we are not careful, it will be sides taken in a world conflict.

It is essential to life on this planet that man gets into the concept of Volitional Science, and that the concept of governing be oriented about property, its definition, its creation, its maintenance, and the respect necessary to accomplish all this. Don't let me fool you that the word property is limited to land and jewelry, it means everything you own, and that means your life, your thoughts and emotions, your inter-relationships, as well as your physical property. Because there are two alternatives here, either we embrace a concept that allows us to exist and move forward, or we will embrace a path of regression, and it's not clear what lies at the end of the path, but it surely isn't an advanced human condition.

Nation Against Nation

We have a funny one here, because a lot of the conflict is not really nation level stuff. Don't tell that to the other guy, it might just swell his head, but then again, it might make him pretty mad (who cares?). Let's examine:

Type 1 is the swelled or (allegedly injured) heads of the countries. Like North Korea, like Iran, here are just two of the many. These guys feel they have legitimate beef, and are expressing themselves. Nowadays though, the expression leads to confrontation, no longer acquiescence. So this one is strictly personal, even on a larger-than-one scale.

Type 2 is the swelled or (allegedly injured) heads of the religious fanatics/warriors. These guys have a different problem. They are either threatened by the popularity of differences, or have been religiously trained (some might call it propagandized or brainwashed, but the problem is haven't we all) to have either no tolerance or have actual hatred of difference. The bad news is that hatred is easy, you look at conditions and find a scapegoat, and if you are impressionable, it is not hard to capitalize on differences to create the façade of oppression. So this one is strictly ideological.

Type 3 is a head butting of economies, which starts out as a protectionist policy and ends up as an isolationist policy. At least it is civilized (when it starts).

Which is the most prevalent is inconsequential; more important, which is the most devastating to human relations? The problem is that anything of this nature produces a schism in relations, and makes the globe a smaller, more dangerous place. And with the shrinkage due to improved transportation and communication, very more dangerous is an understatement. And this one is nationalistic.

OF RELIGION-BASED INTOLERANCE, VIOLENCE, AND HATRED

Lately, the Israeli-Palestinian conflict has mushroomed within the world's awareness to another front, the Israeli-Lebanese conflict. This really has two other components, the Syrian and the Iranian support efforts, which interestingly enough, may really be parts of the cause rather than simply addendums to the actions. The Arab world seems to be full of population that embraces the concept of death, death to anyone and everyone without true regard for any life, in the interest of furthering the goals of hatred and destruction. The Hezbollah fighter and all his/her ilk have been indoctrinated into the cult of the dying since early youth, or have been thoroughly convinced through religious tirades and it's consequential brainwashing of the supremacy of their cause.

So now there are so many fanatical persons added to the fanatical Al-Queda, that it is difficult to consider them inconsequential. Especially after the thwarting of a potential set of attacks that would have blown up a significant number of aircraft scheduled for flight out of England.

The problems for the free world (or the non-fundamentalist Muslim world) is manifold: how to thwart potential attacks, how to eliminate the attackers and potential attackers, how to squelch the development of future attackers. I have listed both attacks and attackers as the problem, recognizing that plans may be in place, and planners are the source of the plans.

Know what I think?

Chasing after leads for potential attacks in development is not a highly probable source of elimination, because there are too many places in the world, too well protected, whose authorities will turn the other way. This will require world cooperation. That means everyone who could be helpful should be involved. That means that sources of support must be removed or converted into un-safe havens for such terrorists. Where are the sources? Why right in close proximity to the terrorists- their neighbors, their friends, their families, their countrymen. Think I'm kidding-believe me I am not.

Internal Strife

This one has a lot of inter-relationships associated with it. The problem is that probably there are several right positions to take on almost any subject. For example, categorize according to religious belief, ethical beliefs, political beliefs, and survival. And how many other nuances are there? In the political realm, drop the pretense and look at survival of the entity. That's really all that needs to be questioned here, because all the others produce diverse and ultimately confusing positions. People moan and groan about so many things. People have strong positions on so many things. "In-fighting" is a natural outgrowth of democracy. In some countries, "in-fighting" is a natural outgrowth simply of polarized positions. I am not sure if there is too much difference between the two, however, I am sure that physical "in-fighting", although effective in a barbaric way, is not a good way. It escalates, it destroys, and it commands retaliation in kind. It kills. Philosophical fighting, wars of words, cut-throat political and financial actions, innuendos, outright propaganda campaigns; these are things man does, maybe even needs to do, because after all, we evolved from lower critters and we have a proud heritage there-from, right? But internal strife for the purposes of this conversation is the things within an entity that create divisiveness. Discussions always start with the easiest reference points, global discussion has to start with what those represented really want. In some governments, that means the desire of the reigning powers speaks loudly, and may in fact be the only voice due to lack of sophistication or voice of the general population. In some countries, such as the United States, there are lots of factions, all given a say, but not necessarily equally. Foreign policy, how others are viewed, how much support is given, how much trade is accommodated, monetary policy, military support treaties, exchanges...no real end to what makes up foreign policy and how it is implemented. Interestingly, if you slice and dice the various views, you will find some on a political note such as Democrat or Republican, some on an ethnic note related to either previous country or race, some on an ideological basis borne of prior experiences, the categories can be broken down in terms of emotion or intellect. This does not include whether the person is "right" or "wrong", since again, who is to decide?

That is currently the case in all the Islamic nations that are in turmoil. The instigation was Osama Ben-Laden and Al Queda, because those entities and their many supporters blatantly pushed into the Western world with violence and hatred. This was not done overnight, because the schools in many areas of Islamic control had been staffed by fundamentalist teachers whose sole and only purpose was to foment hatred. The problem is deeply rooted. Was this never known by Western civilization until the time of 9/11? I think it was known hundreds of years ago, and not monitored in a suitable way. I think that at the time, the nations and leadership thereof were not sophisticated and far-reaching enough to put a suitable watch process into effect. At the time of the League of Nations, there were other interests to watch, such as the consequences of World War I, and after World War II, when the United Nations came into formation, again the focus was on other issues. Blame cannot really be placed, because everyone is a part of the shortfall, even the terrorists are a product of a shortfall, and interestingly, they acknowledge that. So internal strife is a thing that needs to be examined through diplomacy first, because if it can be nipped in the bud, it will not blossom into full out and out struggle.

This doesn't say that a country like the good old US of A is any better. Look at poverty, look at racism, look at religious intolerance, just to name a few. And guess what, each of these subjects breeds internal dissention.

Chapter 4-On The Economy

I am admittedly a capitalist. I relish the idea of trading my labor (physical or mental) as a speculation or an investment for things I desire. Got no problem in putting it out there and seeing what happens. That's venture capitalism at its best. As Ruth Gordon said in Harold and Maude, "Take a chance". So we all know that barter worked its way up to the sophisticated trading techniques of today. And if you can take money or labor and take a profit from the results, then more power to you. In a democratic, capitalist society, going out on a limb is a risk-reward profile to the utmost. As I previously mentioned, so long as there is respect for property, intellectual and physical, then transactions in the free market place are the perfect working of the bargaining/compromising system.

Of course, necessarily there are tremendous swings in the economy due to the laws of supply and demand. Show me something good and new, and you see a short term shining star. Almost immediately comes an entrepreneurship that latches on to a winner, and market forces will bring the value to a happy compromise between seller and buyer. So it goes everywhere. And because we are so electronically interconnected in the world today, there is absolutely no reason why anyone, anywhere, who wants to compete, should not be so allowed to do. Cries of unfair advantage are perfectly fair; they represent the shock of challenge and are sometimes the first response. I think that the most important economic parameter is really management of change, not change itself. I say this because countless times I have seen the chaos and acrimony that ensues from knock-down drag-out competition, and the corresponding low blows that sometimes accompany the effort, such as inter-company spying, extreme governmental subsidies, tariffs, bribery, and the like. I sure have lumped lots of things together, but that is because they have one thing in common, they are all forms of change management through attempts at competitive edge. Curiously, some of these elements have acceptability if suitably practiced, but there needs to be a moral edge to assure that they are really market forces rather than under-handed acts of self-preservation. Who's to draw the line? And, what is the line, what are the criteria, what are the processes and practices that are acceptable? And what punitive action if violated? Guess it gets back to intellectual and physical property. Is spying and bribery unethical-in some societies yes, in some, anything that works is OK. That may put things in the moral realm, or maybe it is the business realm? Wow, what a quandary. That's where a concept of universal morality can be a player. Volitional aspects of interaction are important, and they are a way of conducting oneself.

So where is this going? It starts by saying the globe is a complex place, and human interaction needs to have a common basis for all those who wish to be involved in a global perspective. Gotta jump past the local mores of your 'hood, past the practices of your local governing body. R-E-S-P-E-C-T, Aretha got it right, that is the key word in volitional inter-relationships. In addition, a concept for managing change is critical, as new and different situations are encountered, there needs to be a suitable way of dealing. Interestingly, there are some that don't want to join a global community if they have to modify their behavior. Seems to me that's OK, don't join. Then comes step two, which is about the global community wanting to enter the limited sphere of the non-conformer. That's were the issue arises. So the segmentation, and the need to play a game of "GO", where the territories become bounded, but in this case, let's just say everyone wins by it. Big battle to determine where the boundaries are though, and that has got to play out.

Let's look at energy for a minute, because technology requires energy. There is no other way than to recognize that control of energy source is a key, and the recognition of that means the freedom to live without threat. Because the recognition means that alternative sources are essential- and change management is the only way to navigate through this prickly path. Affluence needs to be tapped and directed into research, and that means unwavering direction towards the goal. Lots of alternatives are possible, a matrix involving potential power availability, cost of development, harnessing, cost of production, cost of setting up logistics/distribution, this matrix should clearly show the viable candidates. Can't believe this hasn't been done, maybe as directed by a government, surely as directed at high corporate levels. So a series of serious sessions is in order to put together a plan. You start the whole process with a mission and values for the group, and then get into strategies for accomplishment. Sounds like a lot of management BS, but let's take a hypothetical look.

Mission- the development of a worldwide, inexpensive set of energy sources.

Values- (behaviors to be used in this task) -the world is the customer, and it is necessary to provide products that can be accessible to all. Under all scenarios and throughout the process of research, development, and production, be sure to recognize the lowest common denominator, the ubiquitous consumer.

What will this all do? It looks at world trade in a different light, because the cost of production is significantly lowered everywhere. It looks at world poverty and elevates the standard of living by making more things accessible more cheaply to all. It looks at OPEC and says you are just another source, be competitive, not monopolistic. It looks at social interaction and offers that all of us are on an equal footing. And growth of the global economy is assured, because limits no longer exist.

One of my personal bugaboos has always been the concept of tariffs. I became sensitized to the damaging impact of the tariff when I realized that as a byproduct, it is a method of reducing affluence. This is in the big picture, certainly not in the miniscule local view. Protecting local industry is the same as protecting motherhood and apple pie, but the problem with the tariff is that it creates a barrier to wealth, not a protection of it. This is because you need to see that the big scale is that a less expensive product means more for your money, more product for the sweat of your brow. And the producers, at a cheaper price, are generating the kind of competition necessary to elevate everyone's wealth, where wealth is defined as accumulation. Takes time for this to work, and that's where managing change is an absolute necessity. The time relates to a bigger picture, one in which the low cost producer's edge slowly dissipates, as low labor costs eventually rise, or as a competitor makes a breakthrough. In response, it might be time to enter another business venture if costs no longer allow competitiveness. Sounds easy, or to some, maybe it sounds tough. Well it is that, but that's the venturing into the world.

What about "from each according to his ability, to each according to his need"? Sound familiar? That's called welfare and socialism, and also communism. It is also a tremendous drag on the concept of free enterprise, because it spreads the wealth unjustly. I just said unjustly, which is a personal prejudice, but my opinion is based on the concept of respect for property, in that each of us converts our worth into our wealth, and only by choice should we offer it to others. Nothing wrong with that (offering to others) by the way, only it must be by choice, not ukase.

The economy is the result of the total interaction methods of its constituents, can't have hateful acts involved, just market forces. But the people populating the societies also drive the economy, and that means the personalities of those who lead. There will always be those who are up front, and by their dynamism, will be the ones who try to mold their surroundings. That's why societal rules are critical, bounds that will ensure that personal gain does not encroach on the property of others beyond their suitable recompense. That means that if you venture, you may or may not gain; but the venturing is yours to do. And that's the world.

Is it our right to grow and expand? Is it anyone's right to accumulate wealth and comfort? The lowest form of human happiness is security-giving up everything else to be assured of food, clothing, and shelter, however minimal. Sort of like the animals, just build around the threats of nature and don't worry about any other aspect of life.

World Trade

Let's talk a little about world trade, which means the privilege to look around and insert your needs into other places, so long as RESPECT is still acknowledged. Taking advantage of a situation is really a negotiation, so long as RESPECT remains a player. What I mean is that if everyone feels they profit, then what's the issue? Do people really offer something to someone else without first deciding if they want to, or if they need to, or if they can pass on what they are offering? OK, in some instances the full gamut of choices is not always accessible to both sides, and that makes things tougher, and the morals of the situation may become dicey. But a world economy is based on everyone being able to play, at the economic level upon which they can act. I'm talking about highly industrialized to highly industrialized by interchange of technical know-how or product. I'm talking about low industrialization to highly industrialized in terms of labor, or low technology output. Also, low to low in terms of the equivalent of barter. Where's the rub-is it benefits, wages, or what? The key is that there is an influx of, or satisfaction for, a need, maybe just the amount necessary to stay alive. Look at standard of living, and see if what appears unfair to one society is really a boon to another.

Well, we also have to look at what happens when there is a disproportionate outflow from one to the other, and when there is a loss in opportunity to one or the other. I'm talking about out-sourcing in this case, a subject I cover when I discuss tariffs. I don't have a lot of sympathy for protectionist philosophy, although I absolutely believe change management is essential to allow smooth transition. And guess what, there is never a GIANT change anyway, it starts small and builds. It is a responsibility to notice.

Affluence comes when work becomes easier, and output becomes less expensive to produce. That is another slow process. The danger is in the potential greed of the brokers. Can't siphon off too much of the interchange or the consequence is loss of fair exchange. That is up to all parties to assure fairness. That can be done with exposure of all the facts of all the transactions. It happened in the US with Enron and many others, in that the highest levels eventually got pinned to the wall. Disclosure on a frequent basis prevents unfairness. It may point out the soft points and the easy entry points, and that's OK; because advantage is where you can get it, and if it doesn't last too long, then press on and keep seeking.

What does this all have to do with Global Economy? Plenty, because it forms the basis for free trade.

You know that in order to improve the economy, there needs to be an opening in the marketplace for more customers. One way is making the product more available to the customer, such as through price reduction. Or at least a change in affordability, which occurs if the customer affluence increases. Another way is to open the marketplace by creating a distribution to places heretofore untapped. That's what world trade is all about- the search for the market. There are three sides to this story, creating the product, selling it, and buying it. So world trade means getting the labor and manufacturing at the least cost, and then finding as many markets to sell as can be found. So here goes the economy, upward spiral because products are cheaper and more available. And the good news, the costs of production and the benefits of selling are spread throughout all economies, all nations. However, there is always resistance to something new, whether in the form of outsourcing, or the introduction of "alien" products to a culture that isn't really ready for them, or in the form of a less expensive product supplanting the existing one. I don't know that there is anything wrong with any of these consequences; I do know that change management of the marketplace is critical to acceptance. Take your time and step back. Not everything is a disaster, world trade and imports means that there is a need. Making a product in a less expensive environment is what business is all about. I remember the Zippo lighter. I remember the Toyota and the Datsun. Each of these examples started out as an inexpensive entry product. At that time, two forces were activated. Threat to the receiving market, and choice for improvement to the creating market. American ingenuity did not shine at that time, instead the big American auto companies made the poor trade that current tooling was too big a reinvestment to begin against the soon to be found competition. And the Japanese companies looked around and said, what does the American market want and need? And the competition continued and so far has culminated in today's market. What's the message? Two-fold: look at the market forces and figure out how to survive. World trade makes that happen, or you end up in the "Bandini" pile.

World Poverty

If I may draw my own paraphrasing from Jared Diamond's book "Guns, Germs, and Steel" - climate has been instrumental in shaping the societies of man. The geometrical pockets of technology originated in the temperate zones, where food and survival where a middle way compromise, not so harsh that the entire waking time was devoted to survival, not so easy that there was no challenge. Well, the good news is that man's nature is both greedy and altruistic, and for whatever reasons, the technological societies look at the less technical as fertile ground for either development or plunder. Whichever it is, there is an interchange, and the undeveloped society sees what the "haves" have, and also looks at itself, the "have-nots", and begins some process of change. Other technical societies also look on, and feel the need to woo into the situation, so that the pressure is applied for weaning the undeveloped area into more favorable arrangements. There are giant swings in the free enterprise system, and the pointy end of the stick, which may be plunder, will eventually shift towards a more stable and mutually beneficial relationship. At least, that is the theory. Once again the trick will eventually be RESPECT, and an appreciation of the intellectual and physical property of all parties.

This process requires patience or insurrection, insurrection being the least positive, because the result is always a new and terrible situation to resolve. It takes a world body perspective to see injustice, to see potential resolution, and to see through the long time span to the working plan's final results. In the interim, we have a major chancre, just sitting and festering, but the seeds of positive change always exist. So what about world poverty? Poverty occurs when the human condition is so low that survival is questionable. Poverty is NOT simply lack of something someone else has. Opportunity is the doorway out of poverty. <u>THERE</u> is the condition that needs tending, because once there is a path out, then it will be used. Here is where the "officials in charge, the leader(s), the elected or selected or appointed", need to be held accountable by a next level. This next level by the way, may be the very people being represented, or it might be some august world body. So world poverty and world trade mix and mingle to create a living, breathing situation, one that has the potential of creating the kinds of change that are beneficial to everyone. Opportunity needs to be defined at the local level however, to insure that it truly has some teeth. Can't just say why don't you become a car mechanic, can't just train someone to be one, if in fact there is no market for the skill. But if you are a big auto company, and you can see untapped human resource, albeit untrained, then introducing a factory and a training program becomes a long-range plan with big payoff. Eventually, the bartered trade of hands-on versus pay of the local employee will rise as the society's standard of living improves. Build a better mousetrap and the world will beat a path to your door. So if the factory is hundreds of miles away, then people will move nearer, housing will start, stores will open, roads will improve. I know this all sounds like wishful thinking, and unless RESPECT for primary and secondary property is maintained, this will be wishful thinking. Because any time someone can put something over on someone else, they will try it.

Impact Of Terrorism On The World Economy

The world economy is awfully big. It encompasses all people, all nations, all kinds of points of view. You can define the world in terms of the property controlled and property output. I want to use that perspective because then a tie-in with the impact of terrorism can easily be drawn. Remember that property is life, accumulation, prerogative to act and react, ideas, almost everything there is. I say almost, because I hate to be absolute in the event that I missed something. In this case I don't believe I have missed anything, because everything, physical or idea, is all there is.

So when we talk about impact of terrorism, immediately look at the two sides, the perpetrators and the recipients. The perpetrators can claim their right to their intellectual property of a credo that pits them against the rest of the world. Pitting is therefore the pivotal issue. As soon as the actions lead to infringement of property rights, then and there is the violation. Consider also that the recipient of the terrorist action has two external foci; one is the receipt of the acts of the perpetrator, the other the wrath due to either real or imagined offenses which caused the terrorist action. Can we march right in and lay down dibs in a culture that has not asked for them? Or extending the thought, if some say OK, at what level before it is OK? Obviously some are deeply offended (read totally pissed), and are striking back because their world is threatened. Just as obviously, no level of compromise was attempted.

Well, now we have a world economy that is extremely sensitized to both sides of this issue, and believe me, both sides need to be recognized. No excuse for the actions taken, the lives lost, the wealth destroyed; absolutely none. Now comes the big thinking process as well as the big reaction process, in the latter, we are responding in kind, in the former, well, I am just not sure that we have a plan in effect (although the physical invasion of Iraq and Afghanistan had the intent of establishing a democratic foothold). Occupation, turnaround, and then withdrawal are the three steps in the "thinking" process. A tip of the iceberg, consisting of a democratic stronghold in a region of secular thinking, is a start.

Both sides are served by this conflict, but at what expense? The whole world is now totally upside down with the realization that modern technology puts anyone in some degree of control. But the "anyone" cannot be unaccountable for his or her actions. Whether it is his or her followers, nation-states, or the whole world, NO ONE can be totally unaccountable. The problem lies in the mission statement that death is the culmination and is an embraced action. What a credo, it is totally closed loop in that whatever is done is rewarded! The world pays dearly for this dedication, because the ratio must be at least 1000 to 1 in terms of impact.

Also, now the terrorist concept, (by the way, the term may not apply to specifically one organization) begins to attract more than the dedicated individual, now it attracts thugs, thieves, misfits, the whole gamut. So in front of our nose is a concept that may or may not have a single dedicated goal. It does have some common results, and those include for the most part, the idea of separation. That is the whole thing isn't it, because the terrorist wants separation, not even with a goal of ransom, not with a goal of compromise, but with the idea of dispersal of unity? Think of it, communication and travel have made the world smaller, it is TIME that is the big common denominator, now we can have a closeness of minutes, and all relating to the time it takes to communicate. So the terrorist is thinking to sever the connection. But what we can do is strengthen it instead. That is what the counter-terrorist approach is all about. We must counter it with a united and consolidated front. It is essential to assure that fragmentation is repaired. It's hard to see a slight fracture almost immediately. Then it is hard to avoid the backlash. But that is what we need to do. To step back and recognize that it is the few, not the many.

A terrible consequence of terrorism is loss of affluence. In some areas this is a really big hit. It fetters the freedom of movement in the world; it erects barriers based on ethnic differences, and raises suspicions based on racial profiling. Then it creates backlash, and takes whole communities and converts them from imbedded citizens into the equivalent of ghetto dwellers. It is a terrible thing, the consequences of mistrust. And again, that's what the terrorist mentality wants-divisiveness, barriers, fear.

Solutions will be long-term and long-time coming. When I look at the make-up of the exposed terrorists, they are diverse. But mostly, I see that years of training and propagandizing were necessary to produce the result. Polarization is imbedded in the training, which starts at a very young age. It is an awful thing to recognize that skewed religion is a source of this cankerous growth within civilized man.

I look at the very recent Israeli withdrawal from Gaza, and it overwhelms me with sorrow. The Israelis actually blew up many of their edifices in an effort to prevent the Palestinians from coming in and doing the same. Surprise, the Palestinians came in and destroyed as much as they could almost immediately. WHY???? So much money and effort was expended in the creation of that wealth, and there it was, transferred free of charge, to be used by the Palestinian government, as they would see fit. And so the ecstatic Palestinian rabble did the honorable thing, they destroyed this "tainted" gift, which by the way, is just concrete, wood, and steel; but of course, it had been touched by Israeli hands, built by Israeli tools, designed by Israeli minds. The joke? Use it, and it is yours-possession is nine-tenths of the law, in this instance, handed to you on a silver platter.

This is part of the terrorist mentality, a part just as terrible as bombing, because it destroys and feeds on itself. Is the solution to eliminate the terrorist? Is the solution to get even? At some point, the solution must be to eliminate the terrorist mentality. Not just contain it, but to put it out of its ecstatic misery and get the concept of death, getting even, and violence, out of our thinking process. Man needs to continue evolving socially, so that interactions are beneficial to both parties. Sounds like negotiation to me.

Energy/Oil Impact

Here's a big one. Oil is a limited resource. This should be making everyone nervous, because in the foreseeable future, oil reserves will be depleted. But, look at the alternatives. They are infinite. What the heck, there is no reason why research can't identify the right solutions. Again, what criteria? Let's start with safe, then accessible and available, then logistically easy, then cheap, then efficient. These are not in any particular order, just that they are characteristics necessary to define an energy source. What's on the shopping list-well, what about the sun, nuclear power, wind, water, gravity, hydrogen, methane, corn stalks and wood, and plenty more. It's all about transition and change. The issue is the gun to your head because right now, we are oil-dependent. I have to wonder, with all the financial power available to governments and to private industry, what in the world is keeping someone from identifying the next world energy source? Makes me pretty upset to think that all the leaderships of the various governments and industries can't get beyond the petty into thinking about the future of the world, and incidentally, the not too distant future in which energy is no longer an arm-twisting blackmailer.

The problem is that each of the entities is independent, and driven by their own forces for their own good; no one is really looking out for anyone else. That is what free enterprise allows, but that same free enterprise is saying keep on looking and you can do better, in this case, for yourself, and serendipitously for the world. Nothing will happen so fast that the infrastructure will collapse, in fact, that very infrastructure can be used as a conduit for the new sources. Fragmented groups are trying, but they do not represent a large enough minority to have major impact. Their efforts fall on opposition ears and are rejected or fought harshly. Security is the lowest form of human happiness, and change is the enemy of security. Boy, is that tough, because deep down, it is true.

My opinion is that realization of a finite supply of oil is a really good thing. Darn it, it SHOULD force us to go for much higher efficiency in terms of power of the source. I really like nuclear energy; it's no different than the sun, except it's local. The problem is containment, and once you just capitalize that term, then you can focus on it and beat it into shape. In the big picture, so long as there is mass, there is nuclear energy potential. But I drift, let's get back to the financial implications of oil as the primary energy source. Now that oil has hit over $4.00 per retail gallon, the free world is starting to get nervous. And, rightly so. Part of the issue is OPEC, and demonstrated by a smaller but very real part, the effect of a Louisiana hurricane, which has cut down the number of wells that are up and running. Oil is a fossil, so that means that the old is supplying the new. Unfair. I say we need to move into technological solutions.

I think the technological solutions are so numerous, that dedicated research will clearly surface several really promising winners. All we need is the right criteria to start with, such as perpetual, safe, present and available, achievable, disposable if necessary, cheap. Maybe some more because I haven't started the exploration yet, but from the concept of System Engineering, the requirements need to be sorted out at the top level first, then flowed down into the subject study. I have found that the requirements can be reassessed if necessary so long as the trace-back is properly conducted, and all the effort is correctly amended. At the onset, this is not a problem, but as the study progresses, oh boy does it get messy if you manipulate the basics. So lots of careful up-front prep insures a nice smooth effort, where this descriptor is quite positive in nature. I believe that studies have been conducted everywhere and by everyone, including think-tanks, governments, and private companies. I believe that the plethora of information available can be used to begin a real effort. Who should run it? Probably a group dedicated to truth, one that may be funded by proprietary interests as identified above, but the funding sources need to be separated from the effort, and the personnel involved need to be evaluated on an independent, results-oriented basis.

I believe that the study needs to recognize social impacts, financial impacts, time frame, etc...

Nowadays we are seeing a spike in gas prices. We are seeing the big oil companies recording record profits, although as has been pointed out, the profits are measured in $$$$billions, but they are only about 8% of gross. Many, many big companies, such as the electronics and computer businesses, are actually registering 15% or higher. So it is inane that the general populace and the general political bureaucrat are bitching and moaning about the cost of gas, when in fact, it its strictly market forces that are causing the rise in prices. Boy, when it comes to the pocketbook and self-interest, frothing at the mouth seems to be the best answer-amazing.

Socialistic Tendencies

This one is really interesting, because the world economy is really a function of the way the pieces run, as well as how they are interconnected. So we have the three ways of viewing the world: free enterprise, socialism, and who cares (laissez-faire). By the way, things in-between that create compromise, cannot be left out, because amazingly enough, politics is compromise, living is compromise. Tell me that you don't trade one thing for another, and I think you will have to stretch pretty far to validate that. Don't forget, we are talking about your life experience, not just a single facet. So when you drive the new Mercedes, are you sure that nothing else was mollified? If you are so wealthy that the dollars involved is not a factor, still, you have made a choice of the type of car, and that means the location of factory, the standards of the company, the repair garage, the gas mileage ticked up. These may sound trivial, but multiply by all the thinking, selecting beings involved, and it is a big factor.

Getting back to the subject, if the pendulum moves towards a socialistic society, it means that the choices and availability of services become less, the up close and personal decisions become more remote, the incentives are severely limited, and the desire to do well becomes thwarted. Take a look at socialized medicine first. You might ask, so what's wrong with everybody having coverage? It isn't that at all. It's all about choices and quality. It's all about the leveling of incentive. Each of us, including those who do not have much, makes choices as to where his /her wealth goes. That could mean food, clothing, shelter; it could mean booze, gambling, women; it could mean that none of these could be afforded.

All right, lets really peel the onion. It starts with people who decide to have kids. That includes the least affluent areas as well as any other. Their peers, or their contemporary ruling class, and thus the social mores of the society, have decisions to make early on that involve the non-affluent within their sphere of influence. Question asked by potential parents- " Is it OK to have kids?"- answer should be yes, and the reason is to be based on the parents' need to project and see if they can raise and place these kids into a self-sustaining situation as they pass into their own recognizance. That's the first of the steps-parents need to insure that progeny can make it. Darn it, that might even mean that welfare breeds welfare. But that situation is one that Welfare can work on to change, in other words, an infrastructure modification sub-set. No matter what country or where, individuals do not have a right to someone else's something. If the parents could not project the self-sufficiency, they should not have had the kids. All the parents need to do is make sure the kids get enough smarts to make a living. How good a living will determine such things as the level of health care. This is not harsh, it is just logic. If some people elect on their own to embellish the system, then the system and its people will benefit. But if a person does not want to share in his/her work effort product (i.e.. salary, earnings, whatever), then that is up to the individual. Again, the responsibility to raise a child belongs with the parents, and the culmination and graduation of that child into the adult world is directly a result of the parents' support. Don't do it if you can't handle it.

Once again, transition and change control are elements that need to be applied. We have a world where the non-sophisticated have done whatever they wished, and tossed the consequences onto anyone else other than themselves. This needs to be recognized and dealt with in ways that are humane yet forward-thinking. So maybe there are welfare roles that must exist in the interim. Maybe the economy needs to be burdened with some sense of handling this condition until it can be stemmed and cauterized. Best effort would be a worldwide agreement, and frankly, that is not a bad way to go. For example, in areas with low standards of living, it requires less to maintain. This translates into each government doing the same percentage of GNP to establish the welfare pool in the area. Along with the pool is the percentage thereof which goes into the mitigation plan, the method of looking ahead towards the elimination of the condition.

Growth

Growth of the economy is dependent on the real conditions of free trade. Its measurement is the value of the dollar or other similar fiat. One might wonder if growth is just proportional to the number of dollars around (by the way, yen, lira, dollars- all the same). I think not, I think it is productivity that makes growth. Productivity can increase affluence, because it produces a less expensive product that then becomes more available. So affluence is the goal, because it produces and is a result of the economic growth required. Feeds in a bootstrap effect, the higher the more. This is simplistic, because we need to burrow down into the society to identify and establish if necessary, the baselines for this to occur.

What is growth in this context? Economic growth is expansion of influence. I think it's that plain and simple. What else translates into money? Growing the size of a company is a way of expanding influence, more jobs, more product, and wider venue is influence, so that's it. First we start with intra-national and watch a product expansion process, which results in more impact through the economics of sales and the entire infrastructure that results in profit. This subject is tied into the economy, so I am sticking with dollars, but influence is also what is going on. Within any one nation, there is a struggle of competing companies to get market share, and that is micro-growth as the entity gets to expand. But eventually, if the nation is not expanding its own influence, there will be a stagnation point where all the product is being utilized, and then status quo ensues. This is where growth must turn outward to international markets, and then the story is a little bit different, but not too much so.

World economy is an exciting thought. I used to think "space economy" at the time the first vehicle made it to the moon. I thought that man could expand into the solar system and beyond, (and still do, by the way) but I think now that first we better learn how to handle our expansions within the various cultures of man before we go where no man has tread before. Frankly, international growth is just an adjunct of intra-national, although rules are different due to legal requirements, due to cultural aspects; to any business that wants to head that way, this is just learning the market and moving into it. Of course, there is the protectionist side, the side that is being "growthed" into, but as I discussed, both sides need to step back and manage the change transition. Management on both sides of any such agreements (and management means governments as well), have got to plan ahead. That becomes the charter and responsibility of the management entities, to look at the trade-offs of market change and to set up a transitional movement that allows a graceful entry, a gentle change process, and a graceful utilization of benefits. So far, I am talking about products and services coming in, because frankly, if the product is not well received, then the venture will fail. Tariffs are not the way to handle this, because that would be where initiatives get stifled. Tariffs may sound like a good transition movement, because they artificially control the absolute desire for the product. The fact that you want something, but it's price puts it within marginal reach, means that the product moves in slowly, and either it gets cheaper thus compensating for tariff (by the way, that won't work if tariffs get continuously and proportionately raised), or a competing non-tariff product is brought into the marketplace. There has got to be a better way to do it. Trying the concept of free market forces allows the big ups and downs of the economy, and if the economy is healthy, it adjusts eventually. The desire to succeed will bring in entrepreneurs with knock-offs, or even a better and cheaper product. In a world market, knock-offs are a bastardizing of the concept of property rights, they themselves are wrong unless there is a business agreement that recognizes the rights of the original. I realize that in order for this to be a worldwide marketplace, there needs to be a significant infrastructure in place to protect the participants. Does this ever happen? I think so, but only in a well-developed and law-abiding nation or agreement of nations. So real growth of the economy requires trust; either in each other, or in a controlling over-system that allows the market to interact, but corrects for violations in the concepts of the marketplace.

Chapter 5-Education

Can anyone tell me why we need it? After all, don't our progeny get stuff from Mom and Dad, and doesn't that mean they can survive, and why the heck do more? Well, just maybe, and of course this may be tongue in cheek, "there are more things in heaven and earth than are dealt with in your philosophy", whomever you are. Start with the point of education- probably means the exposure to things currently not known, or something like that. The reason I would want it that general is that the formal aspect of it needs to include learning and experiences that are beyond what a person gets just swaggering down the streets, and even what is provided by any one individual as a surrogate teacher. Not to say that one individual isn't capable of structuring a formal education process which is complete, but that one individual is not likely to know all that is available. Ditto for expanded group awareness to the family, and even to the neighborhood. Broadening is the key.

Now we need to talk about education from a content point of view- what are the subjects that will be discussed? Full gamut, again depending on interest level, and guess what? On the objective!!! So let's examine some of the possibilities, starting with the young child, who in an ideal situation would have choices like these:

-he or she is at home or in young-child care for some period of time.

-then the transition from full time home to part time introductory school

-then comes the big move to real but elementary school

-at some point the decision to either continue education or go vocational

-if the decision is schooling, then onward and upward to college and maybe graduate school

Hate to say it, but the ideal does not exist for everyone, and besides, that's my ideal, maybe not yours. Described above is a time-line for a specific social set. Variations on this theme come in all sorts, such as income level, religious orientation and its influence, geographical constraints, family background, school/ teachers/equipment availability, student capability and interest.

It is not a given that the parent wishes the child to exceed the station of the parent. Generations of people have forged tight social structures designed to perpetuate the status quo. It takes vision to go beyond that, and sometimes that vision introduces conflict. Ala "Fiddler on the Roof".

Availability

What is guaranteed available is what is picked up informally from exposure. Sometimes it is a very tough juggling act to even get to a place that offers any training of any kind. Sometimes, such places just don't exist or don't offer access. When I talk about availability, that means here in the good old USA. There really is no reason to think that some form of education is not just waiting for exposure everywhere in this country. Quality is a different issue, discussed later, but at least there is something out there for you, and there are laws that require the adult supervisor to take the young mind to the exposure center. That is the start of something big. The kibbutz in Israel was an effort to get kids into a same environment, it's initial purpose was to free the parents from some of the parental tasking and allow the parent to dedicate himself to the general welfare, and allow that general welfare to raise the child. That is similar to the bussing that goes on in this country, where the child is exposed to a different environment than his/her basic neighborhood. Of course, in the case of bussing, there is a severe penalty associated with the travel time to and from the new location that has always bothered me.

In certain backwater areas, in certain geographic locations, in some countries, the possibility of available formal education is nil. Infrastructure is not set up, and even need and desire may not exist.

This is true in poorer areas, and the possibility of rising out of that level of existence is lower than in other places. Yet, there is always the possibility of a plan that modifies the social structure and assures educational availability. That must be a primary goal; otherwise the possibility of rising beyond the surroundings is reduced.

I need to qualify what I have said; I have been focusing mainly on the US. In the rest of the world, I have not done the research to speak in a knowledgeable manner, but I have serious doubts that education is available in many of the less economically fortunate areas, and in fact, believe that some cultures strive to minimize exposure.

Education is the key to departure. That coupled with the desire and (oh yeah) the opportunity, is the necessary set of instigators to move someone from one stratum to another. The obligation of the governing body and the supervising parents is to push the availability, to stress the upward movement. I know that in the early 1900s in the US, immigrant parents held the highest ideals as being an improvement from what they were to what could be for their children. I know that now, in the US, there is a strong push by many parents to get their children to perform in the top percentages of their public school classes, and then to do well in college and grad school. But really, I am talking as well about the kids who come from less education-oriented family groups, especially the lower income groups. Here is a major challenge, maybe not the biggest challenge, but certainly a formidable one.

Availability alone is not the answer; it really does take positive input from the parents, the peers, or the system. Parents and peers are pretty straightforward, but the system is the one that isn't totally in order. One method is what was tried in Israel on the kibbutz- take the children and have them separated from the parents, and educate them from an independent but acceptable source. This was originally done because the settlers had to dedicate full time to running and operating the kibbutz. Another method is bussing, as done in some parts of the US, and I am sure in many low population areas. This method is very inefficient, and in fact, may not provide the desired results because the time spent in traveling eats into the living time. It's original intent was to provide both a "better" academic environment, and to give the recipient an opportunity to see how other segments of the society are structured.

Both of these methods still have a basic receiving area where the child gets the education. In the case of the kibbutz, the child has lost a large portion of personal contact with his parents. So the school environment helps provide the social input. Not much different than private school actually. In the case of bussing, there is no make-up for the lost time on the bus. But since school time is the same, then the family is the time that suffers. The right answer is neighborhood schools that meet standards that produce educated children. One of the goals of every society, no matter how rich or poor, must be to insure that an educational infra-structure is in place so that each and every child is exposed to at least the necessary minimum standards, and an opportunity for furthering the education must be made available for the child that excels.

Don't forget, the human is one of the few creatures that does NOT begin with a fundamental set of survival instincts. There is no ingrained memory, and without the learning process, the child is marginalized. In higher animals, the parent does in fact teach the young the rudiments of survival, but this is in a raw natural environment. Humans have created their societies, their civilizations, and without the proper instruction, survival and upward mobility are not only not easily attainable, but end up insuring the person being pigeonholed into a structure that will hold the person hostage.

Quality

It is possible to rationalize that something is better than nothing. The problem with that is the relativity of such a statement. Take life itself, there is no doubt that quality is a factor. So long as happiness and suffering are part of the equation, (though not necessarily balancing each other, simply as factors), then this becomes a marginal game. Again, bussing is a prime example of the thought process wanting to increase quality. Of course, that does not attack the source. In this case, so much money and time is involved in treating the symptom that there is nothing left to counter the cause. Bussing had two main origins: one to improve quality of education by bringing the student to a higher standard area where a better curriculum is available; the second to expose the student to different social strata thinking. Boy oh boy, talk about dealing with a symptom!! Naïve to think that bringing one mindset into a situation would obviously change it for the better without influencing the other mind set. This will actually result in either complete isolation (which isn't really a possibility) or a mixing of standards that reduces to lowest common denominator. That is not good, not right, not effective.

Quality of education is essential to take the slightly formed mind and energize it. Just being somewhere excites some few, but in general, stimulation of some sort is required.

The concept of the charter school, now in vogue in some areas of Southern California, is that the school takes charge of its own curriculum, and that the money allocated to the school through the system is best spent at the school's discretion, so long as the basics of the district/city/state/federal are satisfied. This begins to move in the direction of quality, in other words, it's a grass roots rebellion to return the school to local control. This is a piece of the pie that will head towards improved quality in education.

Another interesting development is Arnold's intent to impose control on tenure so that if a teacher cannot demonstrate capability, then this is faced head-on. This is another plus that will move the quality of education up a notch. I also read that there is a teacher salary inequity between "good" and "low-income" schools. I don't want to get into the semantics of this, so I will merely note that the inequity is about $1500 to $2000 per year, out of an average salary of about $53000. And the statement is made that that inequity is what is drawing all the "good " teachers to the "good" schools. No, I think part is travel time, part is surely location, part is surely the mind-set of the students, and the mind-set of the parents. And, surprisingly, part is the fact that more experienced teachers have longer tenure, and can more easily transfer to whatever they consider a better school. Now, think about the fact that the more experience, the longer the teacher has been in the system, and therefore, the higher the salary just due to standard COLA or more reviews. Arbitrary pooling of the teachers may put some of the good in some of the low-income areas, but motivation needs to be looked at carefully. If a teacher does not want to be somewhere, then incentive must be applied, or some other method of either enticing the teacher, accepting the teacher's position, or dunning the teacher. Boy, can I get in trouble with the teacher's union? Hope they don't punish me by taking away my education! Notice I said union, not teachers.

Desire For-----

Boy, in almost every single situation I postulate, I find that education is a key player in how society and its members act. I think about my own family background, and I know that education was a key component in our lives. It sharpens the mind's ability to move you forward. I am talking about more than just street smarts, that is an education unto itself, and a highly worthwhile one at that; but guess what, that kind of education helps you deal with what is, and by extension, may (and I mean may) be of assistance in moving along, but I guess I am thinking about an expansion process. That means going beyond, opening new doors of opportunity, being equipped not just to deal with the new, but to relish moving into the new.

So when you are a little kid and you haven't even got a perspective on your environment, let alone the world, that is when the education needs to start. Interestingly, care must be exhibited in what kind of exposure you get, because education envelops you, guides you, directs you, and can limit you. It is quality of education that distinguishes the human from the animal, along with it is the ability to impart and receive that education, but nonetheless, without transmitting the knowledge, the brain follows arbitrary channels, and gets proportionate development of potential. I think each individual does have a desire for some form of education; it is in the form of inquisitiveness. So reach out and touch the environment and learn from the interaction. When it comes to pure mental knowledge, rather than physical knowledge, we have a departure. Here is the abstract presented to the mind that at first has no base for understanding that form of perception. In all of the societies of man, education is made available. It is the degree, the depth, the content; these are the variables that lift us. The little child doesn't know, but as the child grows, the questions can begin, and the thought process begins refinement. If care is not taken to allow this to blossom, we may find a rather stilted outlook.

Take a look at the school system operation in the various neighborhoods, separated by financial worth. Percentage-wise, the children are encouraged more in areas where the parents themselves have a better comprehension of the material and the objectives. There is also a strong drive in the lesser economic areas if the parents and children recognize the path to improving conditions. The definition of improvement is critical here, because moving up could simply mean access to money. Or, it could mean access to the tools that open the door to society's positions through economic improvement.

Having a tough time with this, because no matter what, sets of circumstances define the local reality, not my meanderings. I need to be very careful that I don't overlook the certain realities of existence in which the subjects are enmeshed. So desire for education can be as strong in one person as another, but the content of the education received will be totally different depending on the context. Hitting the heights is possible in both cases, but these heights are not the same, and I cannot be the one to judge. Nor can you.

That means that once again, Volitional Science comes into play, and the definition of property brings in the perspective. Everyone be happy with his or her goals and accomplishments, so long as you have respected everyone else. That means that the education you get serves you well, if the results get you where you want to be.

SOMETHING NEW??-and JUST A BIT OF AN EDUCATIONAL SEED

Well, here we are in Iraq, shades of Viet Nam. Did we really do sufficient and meaningful research and preparation for the invasion that we implemented? I remember Colin Powell saying, "If you break it, it's yours". OK, so we agreed to that part of the deal, but I wonder if we really knew how intense the secular feelings were, and how the societal mind sets of the several coherent societies within the Iraqi state are actually life governing as well as life goals. I think not. And now these segments shine in their blackest ways, and are joined by the opportunist radical terrorists to generate daily destruction and to wear down the general population, the occupation troops, all leaderships, and general support. All of those are trying their very best to overcome, but it is a very difficult road, fraught with the awfulness of death at every turn. Can't ignore it, really can't back away from it, because then the insurgent faction will simply take over. In that case, the seeds of a democratic society can hardly survive in a country steeped in another tradition, enforced by the gun. Hunker down and press forward, that seems to be the only way, and rely on the seeds of innovation to counter the violence.

Hey, wait a minute, since the entire Iraqi situation has received so much press, and that means world press, how come the rest of the world sits by and lets all this go on? So Iraq is now a microcosm of the world's feelings. There are obvious supporters of both the striving for a new form of independence, and those wanting to maintain the old and (presumably) cherished ways. Both factions need to look, but the problem is that the insurgents have taken a totally visceral view, and based on their pride in their approach, it's hard to believe that world-view thinking is a part of their make-up. Yet, who knows, maybe I'm confused, is the goal one of "just let me alone and I'll be happy"? That does not make sense, because the radical Ben-Ladin and faction are still active, and aggressive, and remain a threat to the rest of the world. Those people looked their situation in the eye and concluded it was intolerable and the only solution was annihilation of the perceived threat- the Western world. So there is no stalemate, but there is a path. Humanity is stuck with the perpetual conundrum of resorting to sticks and stones to solve the problem. Bad news, we can't rise above it.

Thinking about it, we can apply the laws of statistics to our population and see clearly why we continue to puff up, posture, and grunt and groan. The distribution of our population follows a normal shape that puts extremes out there at the end, with very low population percentage. This is true in nature, and that means that from birth and heredity, we will have certain shapes to the population characteristics.

The modification is the human condition, wherein man is the only creature that influences his environment; that surrounds himself with his modifications. So the thinking and creative actions of man result in non-standard deviations of the characteristics modified. In this case, call it education, or in the extreme, propaganda. Put a pure young mind into the circumstance, and lo and behold it will come out modified. Simple rule, and there it is. A society dedicated to producing extremists will do so. Not to say that in a democracy we don't produce extremists, they are just democratic extremists. Not necessarily proselytizers, not necessarily fanatics of the democratic way, yet they are supporters. In certain extremist Islamic settings, the product is exactly that, an Islamic Fundamentalist Extremist. Little kids, young minds, dedicated to a way which includes the acceptable (no, desirable) goal of dying for a cause with no regard for the existence and sanctity of life, nor the respect for what I will call primary property, which is your life.

This is very upsetting, especially since so many embrace that ideal. Change is a long way away, a long and torturous path to follow. Herein lies the need for a bigger picture to enfold the smaller one. The smaller picture is you and I, and the rest of the societies that live in the western world. Not such a small picture after all, is it? The bigger picture is all of humanity, because unless this thing gets defused, it will continue to fester and grow until it consumes us all. It's like a cancer, and it needs a confinement and then elimination.

Chapter 6- The Environment

World-Wide

This is more than just a funny situation. We find that as man develops more and more capability to manipulate his environment, he also learns that the effects of either manipulation or just plain activity, are far reaching both in geography and time. Global warming is one example. Nuclear energy is a second. Destruction of the rain forests is a third. This list goes on forever, because "ain't no way" you can do something without it having some effect, and the more global is man, the more is the effect. But man being what he is (and nothing is wrong with that), then the selfish- and profit- motive aspects continue to come to the fore. The perspective is short term, and that is the issue. Well, nations are trying to band together still, and their representatives are aware of the issues, but a country has national interests as primary objectives, and unless the compromises that spell big picture are minimal in impact to these objectives, chances are not good for adopting resolutions. The big picture process is not easy to swallow, and although a big picture plan is easy enough to develop, it's the adaptation and implementation that invoke trepidation. Why? It's easy folks; it's all about proprietary interests.

One thing that I read which impressed me, "the world" does not care what happens, it is a planet with an atmosphere and things alive upon it. So don't talk about saving "the world", rather talk about not damaging our environment, about saving the living. Is there a big difference? I think yes, because instead of looking at a fictitious entity you are looking at yourself, your children, and even the many living and breathing things.

Country-Wide

The environment is a big issue in the United States. I believe that is true because some people are far-sighted, but I am not absolutely sure that all people are far-sighted (Abe Lincoln paraphrased). But you know what? Oil is such a big political football that it has urgent effect on our lives. It means money out of pocket on a daily basis for everyone. Free market forces are at work, but also subtle political overtones. Right now, emerging nations such as Mainland China are exponentially requiring oil consumption. Two ways to handle: one is to let market forces of supply and demand take control, this means long-term price impacts until the producers reach capacity (if they want to); or another market force approach is to get to the emerging user and see if the guy can look at alternate energy sources other than oil. So all of a sudden, nuclear energy sticks out like a sore thumb, but the politics of free use and availability of nuclear power immediately attacks the concept.

In the United States, the "protect the environment" supporters are probably looking too far ahead and forgetting that insidious behavior is in the way. When we can't drill to supplant our needs, we end up even more dependent on business relations abroad, independent of their hidden agendas, if any. So the gang that says keep out of Alaska doesn't really care that no one goes there, that drilling is a minimal impact to the environment, and that not exploiting our resources continues to draw moans and groans at the pumps, which aren't likely to go away, because at best, they are cyclical in nature. On a timeline basis, drilling is earliest; efficient upgrades to oil users is next (although this is a smaller chunk of the answer); and alternative energy sources is third (that means us, and the emerging nations). The reasons for this order of things relates to logistics/infra-structure first, and technology development and subsequent production and logistics third.

But darn it, the lobby for motherhood looks starry eyed at the future and just knows that somehow things will be good for mother earth, even though some of the solutions are not "so bad" anyway.

Joseph K. Goldstein

Business Impacts

The way democracy and free enterprise work, there is a pendulum which swings with the breeze and is the consequence of people's latest causes. There is for sure a need to be aware and minimize impact to the environment from the effects of industrialization, from the effects of war, from the effects of almost everything man does. Because we are a major "impact-or" of anything we touch. So business, in terms of any of the human interactions we perform, has two obligations to the rest of humanity. The first is to do what business' do, and that is to make a profit. The second is a modifier of that profit, and that is to minimize deleterious effects. Looking at the first objective, one way to make that profit is to sell the product at the optimum price to maximize profit intake. Another way is to see what is happening as a result of the product and to benefit from that observation. For example, if the product results in a messed up something, how can that be resolved. Comes to mind the prescription drug industry, which sells the second product to counteract the side effects of the primary product. Of course, that is only a stopgap until the side effects are conquered. Same thing in the environmental world, keep on trucking until you've got it down.

Our way of developing is rather helter-skelter, somewhat up and down, and looks a bit like a ping-pong game. That's what free enterprise is all about. In spite of attempts to consider everything, we don't really have it all covered at first. As the process of progress unfolds, that is when we begin to see some of the unexpected interactions. I read a book by Henry Hazlitt, called "Economics in One Lesson", and in it Hazlitt notes that as soon as you begin controlling something, you will find yourself having to control more and more in order to get where you think you are headed, in fact, eventually, you have made major modification to the original intent, and may end up with a totally different definition of the goal, and a heck of a lot more work than originally planned.

That's one of the reasons drug and bio-type companies spend so much time researching and testing, to see the impacts. That's unfortunately how Lockheed and Rocketdyne ended up in deep "bandini" due to ground pollution, when the chemical constituents of new technology impacted the ground, ground water, the water table, and the lives of people. That's what made Erin Brotkovich when she recognized the Love Canal and other impacts. That is what the tobacco companies are now seeing, especially if they hid the results of research. So frankly, now that liability is being closely assessed on everything, the research must be totally inclusive, long range, and exact. Companies are seeing that now, although unscrupulous ones still exist, but as the common laws are raised in level of sophistication, the companies must see that feedback will catch them. And this has to go international, with teeth, so that finger pointing is eliminated, and that liability is clearly defined up front.

Lotsa companies advertise how environmentally friendly they are, or are acting. It's good publicity, and in fact, if it's truth, it's great business acumen. One would like to think that advertising positively would be the answer, but maybe punitive action also acts as an incentive. We see that in the oversights, the laws, the fines, and the closures. But they all work regionally only, and that could be very locally. And they do not work in concert, if the negative and the positive incentives/de-incentives were to be combined into a public front, then we're cooking. But it will take time to get it going. Push too hard and you start the shutdown before the opportunity to resolve. The bio-techs are an interesting case in point. They needed to research some of their experimental products, but even their best safeguards were not up to a comprehensive protection policy. The spread of any bio-tech experiment into the atmosphere could have unforeseen consequences, and that isn't good. Chasing after a screw-up is a harrowing, expensive, and unrewarding situation. Look at the fluorocarbon effect on the ozone layer. Look at global warming. These are things that were definitely predictable. Hate to think that government oversight is necessary, maybe a better solution would be self-monitoring through an equivalent to government by setting up a panel of experts with authority, sponsored by all the big companies, and watching all the companies. Don't know if this makes more sense than a government board.

Chapter 7-Drug Proliferation

I'm not talking about prescription drugs, which is a topic in itself, but of the hard stuff that is addicting and ruinous, the kind of thing that takes dreams and converts them to nightmares.

I'm not surprising you, I am sure, when I start in on this. The trouble with the stuff is that it is physically and psychologically addicting, and causes a redirection in priorities. This moves the user away from productive society into a downward spiral that ends in a never-never land of disaster.

It does a lot more as well, it cycles all of society into a non-productive mode, the need to counter the negatives of the drug culture, including theft, welfare, loss of personal productivity. It requires the efforts of policing.

There is a question, that if the entire drug culture itself was completely isolated, would it be self-sustaining, could it be basically a segment of society that fended for itself? Could it actually interact acceptably with the rest of society and thus be so treated? I personally think not, because the nature of the dependent people is not a really positive perspective, thus eventually spreading that mind-set and dependency onto the surroundings.

Impact On Society-Financial

There is a monster moral issue in the offing, and come to think about it, there is a monster financial impact as well. Not surprisingly, the entire illegal industry is a mover and shaker because there is so much money and so many people involved. It's crazy, and it's terrible, how people want to try, then want, and finally need the product. Without really knowing the percentages, there is no question that this trade involves a noticeable segment of the population. In affluent areas, the sleaze count is low, but as you move into lower income arenas, the effect is much larger. It comes down to why people want this, and eventually how they deal with what they can get. But the fact remains that a noticeable percentage of the GNP is associated with drugs. And this money is off the books, totally, so it doesn't produce its fair share of market value. It produces a spin-off that actually does influence the economy, but at a very inefficient level, as well as wrecking havoc with lives, and being a massive decrement to productivity.

This is also another very interesting spin-off effect; the volume of money that moves through the society for drug use is horrific. The money is re-directed away from the user, into the hands of the dealer and distributor culture. Some small percentage also gets back to the grower. But all of this is a terrible burden. Firstly, the money is off the books, so the transactions never get recorded or attached in any way (that means taxed). Second, there is a very large component of the law dedicated to eliminating this entire sub-culture, and so money spent on law enforcement, which by the way, is non-productive to start with, is siphoned off into the great unknown of non-productivity. And thirdly, as the habit grows, or even if it doesn't grow but just sits at some level, there is a tremendous component of crime that springs up to support the user (unless the user is very wealthy, and then the siphoning is still insidious because the wealth goes underground into illegal productivity). This crime hits you and me right between the eyes, in terms of theft, theft insurance payments, and the black market industry of selling the stolen products. I remember a long time back, when I could have gotten a stolen color TV for 20 cents on the dollar. That's a hard decision to turn down, and I have to tell you, it was not easy to just say no. I don't know if any of that was drug related or simply theft related, but it all stank.

Impact On Society-Citizen Lives

Drugs have a place, and that is within a context. Andrew Weil's "The Natural Mind" had it right- it is set and setting. I do not feel good about any forms of physical, mental, or emotional addiction or dependencies that warp the way of living. Some people don't really mind, but in the background is either a real or suppressed awareness of impact. That's the part of impact that hurts. Anything non-productive takes away from affluence, and frankly, I think affluence is the human goal. Makes sense to me, that the objective is to surround yourself with what makes you happy, that could be physical property, human company, the tools of thought, who knows?

But when you get into a drug cultural impact, then things start getting messed up. It starts with the need to direct your effort towards the production of wealth to be used to obtain the drugs, and in this case, that could be either medicinal or recreational (at least at first, in the minds of the deluded). Medicinal by definition is protecting and prolonging quality of life, while recreational is loosely defined as enhancing or escaping. Both forms can be addictive in nature; the medicinal becomes addictive whether that is physical or simply a requirement to maintain. In either case, you are involved and enmeshed. I have to put the medicinal away, because the only reason people use it is to stay alive and functional. However, the effects on your life of what are called recreational drugs, or the ones labeled hard-core, there is where the problems lie. I don't know from first hand experience, so my knowledge is my own fabrication based on what I have seen, heard, read.

Attack must be in an orderly format, starting with why certain things are illegal and what does that mean? First, are the things bad for you, or why have they been made illegal? I am not condoning anything by the way, just beginning an inquiry into the establishment of the various statuses of the specific drugs. It is not universally accepted that drugs are bad, however, it is recognized by a large percentage of humanity that use and dependence are a major sociological problem. I read about the Indians of Peru chewing coca leaves their whole lives, thereby incorporating that dependence into their existence. Again I am reminded of Andrew Weil's "The Natural Mind", and his concept of "set and setting". There is a situation where the society and its rules have been established recognizing a natural part that in their opinion enhances their lives, rather than tears it down. I think that the high altitude, the cold climate, the conditions of life, all have contributed towards such a solution. Is it the best one? Especially recognizing that other same environment societies have evolved along different solutions? There are always several ways to solve any situational issue, and in this case, the use of a plentiful natural substance became the methodology of choice. This speaks to setting.

However, set is a different issue. In cultures in which drugs are introduced, rather than evolved, there needs to be a set of rules governing use. I don't mean government rules, I mean societal ones. This is where the problems arise. Things become recreational without societal controls, without societal mores, and this means out of control. Altered states of consciousness are sought after within all societies, whether by meditation, ecstatic mind-sets through forms of depravation, or through use of controlled substances, man can achieve the altered state. How that is entered, how that is used, therein lies the rub, My Dear Watson. Of course, use of opiates and their subsequent dependence, is of another nature. Key is the subsequent dependence. I don't think anyone starts out wanting to be dependent; they only want the altered state, for whatever reason. Again, if medically required, then that is a sub-set that is not part of this inquiry. So drugs are either a way of life, or a stepping-stone, either moving towards a dangerous usage, or supporting that dangerous usage in others.

Begin at the beginning. Drugs -"the opiate of the masses". Absolutely, it allows a dangerous escape from conditions. The first reference is "conditions". If conditions were right, there would be less (or perhaps even no) drug use/need/ dependency. Attack the conditions! They include poverty, despair, fear, laziness, and keep going. The drug becomes the easiest way out of conditions. The lowest form of human "happiness". But it really isn't that because it may quickly replace one set of conditions with another. But (you argue!!), what if no dependency arises, what's the rub? And you know what? You have a point, except that "what if " is a big scary. Also, unless a regulatory system is initiated, what would keep the drug infrastructure from tipping the "unaffected" further, and then the "susceptible". And guess what, that is exactly what has happened.

Quickly, the non-affluent fall into a bad and dependent situation, whether actual physical dependency or psychological dependency doesn't matter, because again, it shifts the priorities and manipulates the segment of society. The affluent are conceivably better off, especially if they can stay on the fringe, then all that happens is it reduces the affluence by an acceptable number. But it does change the perspective nonetheless. The thing is insidious, the way it infiltrates and then destroys.

Chapter 8-Pregnancy, Birth, Old Age, And Death

This is one of the later chapters time-wise in terms of writing this book, put in because of very personal reasons. Of course, you probably realize that everything in this book is put in for personal reasons, and many with an additional stomach grinding urgency. Well the Pregnancy part really has to do with taking responsibility, the Birth part with the consequences of that responsibility, Old Age with a recognition that life is a continuum, and the Death part because death is just a part of life that must be experienced and accepted with the same aplomb as was your youth when you were a teen-ager.

Heard a joke once, in the form of a rhyme, and it stuck with me because it really accentuated a moral position.

"Said the good little girl to the bad little girl

Is an hour's pleasure worth a life of shame?

Said the bad little girl to the good little girl

How do you make it last an hour?"

Well, that's really what the Pregnancy and Birth thing are all about-everyone knows it, but some don't do anything about it. The issue is one of responsibility. Once you set a path, amazingly you find that along it are the consequences. I'd like to think that people look beyond the end of their nose (as my father used to say), but frankly, when it comes to this kind of stuff, sometimes our brains aren't doing the thinking. So that comes to the Birth part of the story, which by the way, is one of several alternative consequences, because there are ways to intercept that aspect of the cycle. There are natural and fabricated methods of preventing pregnancy, and everyone can embrace some form of that- starting with abstention, moving on to rhythm, stepping forward into combos of natural herbs, (notice so far that these are natural methods, all, with the intent of offering technique that is not offensive to anyone). Then we get into the man-enhanced generation of preventative techniques. These have moved along through condoms to diaphragms, to IUD's, to many varieties of pills including the after-morning variety. These all are mentioned because darn it, there are ways to avoid the physical consequence called an active pregnancy. Well, man has recognized that being the only creature on earth that exhibits sexual desire as a whim as opposed to at nature's call, this then is a short circuit to the natural flow of things. And surprise, the desire and the act often occur with a culmination in Pregnancy. I know this isn't new stuff, as a matter of fact, it has to be dull and boring. But it is essential to lay out the societal issues caused by man's desires and potentially unwanted consequences. You could say "what you sow, so shall ye reap the harvest thereof." But in a less than perfect world, sometimes the harvest skews things so afar that living with it puts more of a burden on the person and more burden on the offspring than is appropriate.

P.S.- I know that the word "appropriate" here is such a loose statement of consequence that it is in itself inappropriate.

What I am getting to is that the mind of man includes intellect that recognizes that if there could be a way out of an unwanted situation, then it could be explored. If you look at it in moral terms, you see that first of all, morality itself has been either defined by or embraced by man with its derivation based on societal survival, which is after all, what religion is all about. So here is a moral standard that says killing another is not good. Delving into that, we discover that situations creating a condition where killing can occur are also not good. So therefore come more commandments that essentially are part of a moral code that governs man's actions. And goodness prevails. Occam's Razor says that the simplest solution is the best solution. But it must be applied at various levels. You need to go and relate the condition to the rule and see if they match, both in context and resolution. You need to think about whether new innovations can fit within the context. Guess what, abortion is a thing that's been around for thousands of years in terms of primitive solutions, and now all the way to today's most modern techniques.

Should abortion be performed? Clearly yes, given certain circumstances that might prove dangerous to life if abortion did not occur. That means life of the mother, and of the fetus.

Let's look at the morality of the whole scheme of life:

I see a natural, physical cycle that absolutely operates autonomously, male + female +estrus = baby. It's autonomous, because strictly operating on the physical level of it, this equation will produce results. And life is a wonderful, fulfilling experience. Male and female of any species have existed because within the gene-set are the nurturing instincts that assure survival of the species. This is the animal world, and we are a part of it- no morality yet, just hereditary characteristics.

I also see an emotional component. This one starts within the natural physical cycle, because having emotion is a consequence of our inherited gene structure.

I also see a moral component. Moral, by the way, is not necessarily religious. Because religion, by it simply having a different moniker than morality, and that having been placed on it by the religious, is not the same thing. Religion has added additional requirements, and eliminated many as well. This is one of the dimensions that is giving us all so much trouble.

I also see a financial component. Financial is another word for being able to physically cope, because the financial arm is just a translation of the ability to produce something wanted by someone else.

Well, getting back to abortion, and coupled with birth. Abortion independent of birth relates to a discomfort with a change in condition from non-pregnant to pregnant. Abortion dependent on birth relates to discomfort during carriage, change of physical and possibly financial condition during carriage, the experience of birth, the desire to establish a mother-child relationship starting with birth, through nursing, into childhood, culminating in release of responsibility at the appropriate age, or possibly, desire to divest of the baby through adoption.

Pregnancy

Let's start out this process with "getting in trouble". My opinion is that sex is a fine and wonderful part of humanity. It obviously is an important part of the animal world, because it assures survival of the species. In humanity, we have moved from survival to the loftier goal of pleasure. Remember "Terminal Man" by Michael Chrichton? Imbedded electrical connections that were intended to issue reprimanding shocks at improper behavior? Well, turned out that the body came to like the shocks, and so sought out the consequences of the shocks (which became pleasurable), and so re-enforced the bad behavior. Chaos theory says life will adjust, and so it did. Well, look at sex, and tell me if in the big picture, as man's chemistry developed, whether nature's survival plan got altered by man's developing intellect and capabilities, and viola, we have unwanted pregnancy as a consequence of the act of procreation. We do a credible job in some places to inform the uninitiated that sex has consequences. That is not the problem, although the job is left to the family in many other places. The real problem is that even though armed with such knowledge, the urge to have sex (which is actually nature's urge for species survival), is soooo strong that it literally takes your breath away, as well as your intellect. So mankind created two alternatives, one is the condom and the diaphragm, with the shortfall that you better stop what you are doing, run around and get your contraceptive, and then re-engage. The second is any of the various forms of birth control pills, and these do the job. They may have side effects, but they do work. Morning-after pills are a weak third, but they are also available. So there is really no reason why sex HAS to produce pregnancies, except for the cost of the contraceptive devices.

& Abortion

Well, all of the above is pure intellect unless embraced, and the hormones are sometimes momentarily just too strong for the embracing. So we got union and we get pregnant. Now comes the comeuppance, and the time for rational or irrational, emotion laden or not, decisions.

Economics, life style, life plans, emotional attachments, maturity- keep going, and we get to the issues that petrify so many of us at the thought that the pregnancy is unwanted.

We talk about abortion as a form of death, and surely it is an interruption of a life process. But it goes along with the territory of being a human being, it goes along with choices we make every day. Natural selection results in self-preservation, part of that being that the race (human) is best served by procreation, sort of a follow on to Darwinian Survival. That came about in a moral societal mode, and got wrapped around into a religious mode. Well, I personally don't know the right answer, I know a relative one for me. Take a look at the way various cultures handle the concept of family. In a rough environment, the weak were weeded out, either by that very environment or by the cultural mores which allowed that the weak either wouldn't make it, or that they were a problem for the family. Abortion also was a method for just plain unwanted, and all the agony that it imposed on those who knew, was essentially self-imposed. I think that is OK, because it allows a balance. The saving grace is that if done correctly, an abortion does not physically impact the ability to carry children.

Old Age

All these things happen. We're born, we grow and experience, we continue aging, and then we transition through death. We see the body going through the process, and well it should, because the body is the tie-in to the phenomenal world, and it is exposed to the amazingly beautiful process of entropy. Entropy is what the phenomenal world is about. Remember the artichoke? Well, it is entropy in action- the move from order to disorder as we go about the process of eating it. That is what life is about on this plane. What should we do about the aging process, since it fits in so well with the flow of things? We are in the process of separation from the body as it approaches melt-down. Even the confusion of the mind as time goes on- whether we see it as Alzheimer's, or just wearing out, the process is one of extraction from the intensity of the phenomenal experience towards the next phase. Don't really know if the next phase, commonly called Death, is one of nothingness, or new experiences. But do know that the process of aging, approaching old age, is a very gradual letdown. Perhaps it should be more abrupt, thus allowing a quick paradigm shift at the approach of the end of this consciousness. On the other hand, the human being is able to adjust, so the slow deterioration picks away, but doesn't destroy. It is the end that ends it. Surely the aggravation of existing with the physical deterioration could be relieved, but the question is whether that is necessary, or should it remain a slow accommodating process that results in a feeble ending.

Death

Whadda ya think? Everybody's got to have a position, an opinion, some subjectively defined evaluation of what it means to face, experience death, and then experience the next phase, if any. I believe that this will be more what you like than what you know; in the case of "belief", which is really the result of constant imbuement with doctrine, that is a subset of what you like. There have been situations where people claim to have been there, done that. I will not trivialize those reports, because they represent another input, same as all the other inputs, in this case, with different credentials is all.

We over-rate the experience because too many of us fear the transition. For many, approaching death begins a gut-wrenching agony of wondering if we really had it together during this lifetime cycle. The concept of yin-yang is an all-pervading possibility. Take a look at various religious beliefs and they boil down to karma for most of the Eastern Mystic religions, and to heaven and hell for the Judeo-Christian religions. Once out of the religious sphere, there are entire philosophical schools that look at belief and non-belief.

I think that by the time anyone begins thinking about death and hereafter, it is pretty late to make changes in any of the factors believed to influence fate. On the other hand, if your life interpretation includes recognition of current deeds and behavior, then you've got your work cut out for you at a pivotal time.

But what about it? Now that the event is approaching, there is no avoidance of its reality. By it, I mean the event of dying. So everyone needs to step back and confront this reality and accept the upcoming outcome. One of the things that has always excited me about the Laws of Karma is that the consequence of an act can always be two-fold. In one instance, you get the direct result of the act, such as evil for evil. But in the other instance, you get the opposite, such as a requirement to do good after you have done evil. These are not reward/punishment views, they are strictly responsive reactions if you so believe. Very simple way to look at it, and very satisfying (at least, to me). So, even though Death can be considered a transition, into <u>what ?</u> is still the main question. There is limbo, there is oblivion, there is heaven, there is hell, there is rebirth, there is re-incarnation. Every one of these is a possibility, and I am sure there are some more I haven't listed.

I also think that death needs to be discussed relative to some societies satisfaction in the martyrdom of their most zealous advocates. I am talking about suicide bombers, who in the name of their religion, will sacrifice their lives, their future, in the name of their belief. This is one of the enigmas of today's world, such a firm grasp onto what is considered "the very best" that nothing else is important. I personally think that we are here to experience this earth and these societies, and that other personal goals and challenges are a part of the process. Time out, don't think I mean that there are any exclusions, because everything is important in the big picture, because each of us is a part of it.

What I embrace is a karmic principle, and that as we flow through our processes, we are cloaking ourselves in the karmic stream. We switch at will, we watch and experience as it is unfolding. And we absorb, continuously, and we grow. Because, although one thing was not right, many others may be, and so we experience it all, and we react, and we absorb. So when death comes knocking, it is not a big deal. We have left it all behind.

This may seem a little far-fetched, or way out, or something like that, but remember, we are all floating along in life, experiencing it and developing as we experience, even the most hard core of us is not really impervious to life experiences.

I am not so sure about vestal virgins, either male or female, as an end product to the dying process.

Chapter 9- Illegal Immigration

Some might wonder, so what?- this is an issue for each and every country to deal with, as they will. I agree. So what's the beef? It's simple, and it is the word illegal. That means that a group (the inhabitants of a country, or less democratically, the rulers of a country), is internally in agreement that certain limits exist. In this case, they are the rules for the granting of citizenship. Maybe you don't like these limits, and so through some sort of due process, they can be changed. In a majority rules situation, that may be all it takes, but whatever the process, there needs to be one.

It is inappropriate to hold a gun to someone's head and say "gimme". That is the case when a citizen's tax dollars are appropriated for uses not sanctioned. So long as the word illegal is validly applied to a person's status, then there is just cause for questioning the use of taxpayer dollars to support anything but the removal of that illegitimacy. And that means removal of the cause of that status, either through policy change, or through enforcement of the rules of that policy.

No one is objecting to concurrence that a worker can enter legally for the purpose of work, or that a person can apply for legal citizenship. No issue at all with either of those. No problem with trying to better oneself, the issue is doing this without the concurrence of the supporting system and the supporting constituency. If a "recipient" can obtain sponsorship and full responsibility for their support from a donor(s), and with a plan in place to wean such persons into eventual self-sufficiency, then suitable legislation could be provided to support such a program, if the general population so decided. This would mean that eventual citizenship is in the offing for people who want it. Trouble is, nothing is purely black or white. This means that for such a primary law to be enacted, there will be thousands of codicils, riders, amendments, sub-paragraphs, etc… to recognize every possible exception to the rule. This is not good. This should not be done in that manner, because immediately it obviates the primary law through a process of pollution. No kidding, many of the potential exceptions would be worthy of consideration, but they can't be placed on the agenda without the politics of "us too" barging in.

History is exactly a valid reference. Perspective is the reality that needs to be applied to clearly define the direction. Consider the US. In the past, let's say 100 years or so, many European immigrants came to this country. They came for economic, religious, political reasons. They all wanted the same as anyone else-opportunity to do well. This meant working with a goal towards bettering themselves and their children. Is this different than today? It is, because when they came in the past, it was through Ellis Island or other immigration points, with designated sponsors who assured a job for the immigrant. It was with a level of legality created by the law. Sure, some may have stretched the truth, but they all showed up, were documented, and began a life.

That is not what is happening now. Illegal immigrants means the process is reversed, and busted as well. People come in without any appropriate legal pathway, and remain a shadow population, except that where before there were very few monetary stipends available to early immigrants, now the illegal immigrant asks for and gets tremendous amounts of support that is inappropriately given. This is a form of reverse charity, wherein instead of it being given willingly, it is taken. This needs to be re-examined and corrected. Herein lies the dilemma. Once here, should the illegal alien be given any of the rights and privileges of a citizen? Remember, one of the draws is that the answer has been yes. In addition to trading labor for more dollars than available in the home country, here come all the various benefits of the system.

The problem is at the source, at the immigrant's home country, and the standard of living and capability to live needs to be improved there, not drawn-down here. There are methods of nation-to-nation communication, financing, and investment between various countries. There are private monies, which can be invested to improve the conditions of another nation through business transactions. There are even ways for those in sympathy to funnel funds to individuals in another country so that these funds become personal investments to aid economic growth.

Interesting, that in May of 2006, a series of demonstrations was conducted supporting the "Immigrant Cause". At that point, it was strictly focused on illegal immigration and potential legislation. So who is it that is demonstrating. Firstly, it is the Latino population, supplemented in small degree by other immigrant cultures. Secondly, it is the illegal-status people themselves. Thirdly, there are morally and religiously oriented individuals. Fourthly, everyone else.

Well, you know what? I absolutely have no level of support in me for the illegal portion of the faction and the situation. As I have said before, and will say further on in this effort, I think transition is the necessary thought process, and so I don't think a black and white solution of throw the bums out or let's give amnesty is in any way a solution. I think it involves recognition of those with long term history here, and consideration of that status as well as some punitive consequences to the original and still not-changed condition.

Saw an interesting "Mallard Fillmore" cartoon. Phone call to Vicente Fox, president of Mexico: Hello? President Fox? Hi...uh... I and 20 million of my closest friends would like to come live in your country, use your schools, hospitals and social services for free, but keep our own language and culture....

Now...we can't have a serious discussion until you stop laughing, sir..."

OK-now I have to step back, and recognize that everything is multi-sided. In this case, the fact that illegal aliens were not immediately removed allowed that they establish lives and presence here. That means that the US is culpable to that degree. And in keeping with the concept of smooth transition being the right way to manage change, then I see that the US has to develop a "transition-out" plan. This means a method to stop further illegal entry, a method to remove the illegality of those selected, and a retribution/punitive schemology for those who will have the stigma eventually removed.

Cost Of Services

I personally am freaking out at the cost of any government services; it doesn't really matter to whom they go. The only way I don't get upset is when I know there is fair and honest competition in the field, and then I think, well, maybe a proprietary interest is in the running. I don't really have a problem with government employees, only with some of the types of jobs, and then the mind-set that fills them. The problem gets down to politics, the way of moving from the proprietary to the non-committed. But I want to move on to the sub-set of services made available to non-citizens. If there were a cost that had to be paid that would allow the service to be self-supporting, who could object? But if it is subsidized, then there is a problem, at least with me there is. Because we start out with the illegal status, and that means you don't belong until your status is defined as legal. That's when you fit in, not before. Before: you are a fringe item, not nameless, because you have dignity as a person, but where is that dignity when you slipped into the system? I won't listen to excuses for the motherhood side of things if the illegal status places a burden on me. By the way, me is you, too.

Ok, so what to do about it? Starting out, there needs to be better control of the entry of the illegal individuals. Secondly, there needs to be a way to say "no" to the request for services for which the party is not eligible. After all, think about you or me walking up to someone and saying "gimme". First, you would have to prove you are who you are, then prove your eligibility, then fill out the forms, then get a critical review, then get turned down because you have qualifications other than those necessary for fitting into the system. So an illegal alien-how does such a person fit into the system? Again, illegal is the key word here.

BUT, you say, that is inhumane to deny certain services, such as health care. Oh yeah, again, if I walked into any place and said I won't (be able to) pay, guess how far I'd get. After all, this is a free enterprise, competitive society in which we live. Everyone is given the ability to enter the system legally, then to work to convert his or her capabilities into a tradable commodity such as money, and then to spend according to desire and need. Buy your health care, rent your home; all the normal things it takes to make a life.

So let's get back to health-if you have illegal status, then if you need the "system" in order to avert life-threatening conditions, OK---- ONCE. You have now registered as illegal, and now comes part two, which is to handle that status, and that means the illegal person as well as the state. This kind of solution is certainly humane, because no one is denied necessity. Also, it puts the person in the position of recognizing that he/she/they must now forever remain within the illegal underground unless they try to change that status. Now we get into a whole different set of circumstances and conditions (which are a part of another section.)

Part of the trouble is that there is no question that anyone who works is satisfying a societal need. Someone has work to be done and money to pay for it. And the least common denominator is the cost of doing the labor, and the cheapest price for acceptable quality is the out and out winner.

Impact On Law And Order

Oh boy, is this a subject or what? Once the word illegal comes along, you need to break that down into two discreet parts for the view on how a person conducts himself. Lets go black and white, which really means law-abiding or not. So first, recognize that if a person is here illegally, then by rights, any brush with law and order should turn up a giant flag. "Sure, that always happens."

But this is not the root of the problem; it is dealing with a symptom. The problem is associated with the illegal entry of individuals. That is what must be addressed first. Plug the holes, and then deal with the internal issues of those who entered illegally. By the way, everything is identified as change, so change management is the essential ingredient to assure that there is an effective methodology put into place. The entry of "illegals" is easily although expensively stemmed by the application of physical controls. With all our technology, there is no doubt a way to prevent illegal entry. Whether that is through IR/other mechanism cameras throughout the border zones, or the need for bio-card issuance that allows subsequent challenge and check within the borders, some methodology can be assured. The former is the easiest way to deal with entry issues, the latter means you will be identified at a later date as well as it being a method of tracking down current illegal entrants.

Law and order on this subject means coming into compliance with the law. By the way, illegal encompasses not only those who wish to enter as immigrants, but also those who would come here to do harm. This second category is what the order part is all about.

But law and order has another component, and that is the enforcement thereof. As I mention, just placing the law on the books does not insure order. That is where the sovereignty item becomes a player. If you want something, you have to get it. Get it? That means buckling down seriously and stopping the offenders, using the law to apprehend, and using the law's punishment to always demonstrate the seriousness of offense. So if that isn't done, that is exactly what position we are in. Here we now have a plethora of illegal people, I don't even want to call them "immigrants", that are demanding "rights", and a tremendous amount of ethnic support also screaming demands. As well, they have jumped beyond the illegal aspect and are touting the morality of not providing.

Well, we made an error, and we need to take stock at this moment, and balance all the past actions and decisions and move forward. Change control would best be served by minimizing the damage and the offenses and just plug the legal and physical holes from this point on.

Impact On Sovereignty

Wow, lookee here. Is a country allowed to call itself a country? And if so, then are there in fact borders that define the geography of the country. Also, by the way, can this country define its own laws? Two-edged sword here, keep out and keep in. Morality is a player, but not a factor. In that I mean that morality is relative and a choice as well, so if we really believe in sovereignty, then we must accept whatever is going on. But that is not really the case, there are many situations wherein conditions became intolerable and threatening to (some of) the world's governments, and as a result action was taken. Semi-recent history includes Nazi Germany, Afghanistan, Iraq. But going back to the subject, which is illegal immigration, there should be no flaunting of this loophole. First of all, unless and until the laws are changed, they are the law of the land, and people who look the other way weaken the land with this action. This means the immigrant as well as the citizen. In a democracy, the struggle to bring a majority or a vocal minority position to the forefront is both expected and accepted.

It is a testimony to a country that people are literally "dying to get in". However, it is also a major burden to find that such people, entering without sanction, end up creating an entire subculture that lives outside and beyond the law of the land. It is not acceptable, it flaunts the very standards that the country has raised, and citizenry supporting the acceptability of "illegals" are putting other agendas before the valid one in contention. Again, transition is the key to a suitable solution.

Impact On The Foundations Of Our Society

"Give me your tired, your poor, and your homeless" has been a byword and credo of America. It still is, and there has always been a codicil based on immigration quotas and limits. Today is different, because in the past the country needed expanding population and the give and take was slightly different. At that time, the new immigrant offered himself as a body of labor and got only wages in return. The shadow society was essentially self-contained. Now however, the shadow society has expectations, and they impact the rest of society in big ways. This includes wages, welfare, benefits, health care, schooling.... the problem now is that the percentage has reached a critical mass that is affecting the fabric of society. It is reducing available wealth.

Impact on society is much more than the simplistic in or out. The United States has legal methods to deal with conditions that are in violation of law. The foundation of the country is law, and if there is sufficiency to support change, change can be accomplished. Look at Arnold's attempts, which are in process as I write, the public elections to bypass the legislature. Let the people decide if that is the necessary condition to resolve this as an issue.

Illegality is not the right answer, the concept of tagging the "illegals" and then allowing them to continue as was, but to totally restrict their access to benefits, is a reasonable approach, albeit there will be many who see it as immoral or unfair, or something akin to that genre. If this is not an acceptable methodology, then removal is the next alternative. The last alternative (status quo) is not acceptable, because the influx is growing and the financial burdens to the state (read you and I) are increasing exponentially.

Chapter 10-Hurricane At Large

Something happened in Louisiana, in New Orleans. Hurricane Katrina shouted that it was coming, and surprisingly it came. Well, we all saw the devastation it caused, and that after it had actually reduced to level 3 or 4 rather than the predicted level 5. But that devastation had three important issues associated with it. The before, the during, and the after. That's what we saw worldwide through the eyes of the television cameras. This thing needs to be discussed, and I'm sure it has, by everyone, and it needs to be seen as a lesson as poignant as the 9/11 tragedy. That one had it's before, during and after as well. So here goes, and frankly, although I have opinions, I will try to hold passion at bay.

It starts with the past, a relatively long ago past, the founding of the city of New Orleans. At the time, it was known that the city would be below sea level, thereby putting the design in a rather unique position. Dikes and levies, and swamps and natural geographical conditions all came into play in the effort to develop a modicum of safety, although frankly, at the time of founding, there was not a highly scientific capability, just the developing hodge-podge associated with trade in a delta, and growth of the city. So the city grew and prospered, and as time went on and sophistication increased, awareness of the vulnerability of the city became more apparent. Enough of that background, because it is just that, and flogging that dead horse just ain't useful.

The real situation is that there are four political bodies that relate to New Orleans. They are the city, the county, the state, and the nation. (Not counting the citizens themselves). Starting with the city, there we find the most involved, the stakeholders, and the proprietary interest-ers. So as time went on, the vulnerabilities of the city were well known to the elected officials, and therein lies the first and primary responsibility: both to developing a protective capability, and to establishing a workable warning system.

Joseph K. Goldstein

Flash About Flood-Sept. 6, 2005

Something strange is going on. It's mainly on the TV News, but Oprah just picked it up, or notched it up. She called what went on in New Orleans a "travesty". She is very upset with how did all this happen, and has implied that there is a question as to whether the fact that the flood-affected are mainly black had an impact on the way things have and are playing out. Summary of what I saw chronologically:

1-the hurricane was predicted as heading towards New Orleans, and would hit in 2 to 3 days. This allowed some time to prepare in some manner.

2-the hurricane hits, and as everyone felt, it was a 3 to 4 vs. the originally predicted 5 level. This trigger would ratchet various aid organizations to be on the ready and on the go.

3-many people evacuated themselves, many chose to stay, and many couldn't get out of town. First breakdown because why hadn't the city at least gotten it's bus drivers, its trucks, etc. in line?

4-an Evacuation Center was designated (at the Convention Center?) and at the large Superdome. These locations were pre-planned by the earlier Disaster Committees, and were waiting to be staffed, manned, and stuffed with supplies.

5-the levee gave in for 200 feet of length, and flooded New Orleans from 8 to 20 feet of water height. Of course this was not planned, but since knowledge of levee condition was already known, such failure should have been within the bigger plan.

6-not sure how many city/state/federal officials and personnel were in position at this time; it was only about the second day.

7-started getting sporadic reports of deaths, of shooting, of looting

8-started getting reports of poor conditions in the Superdome, but not of anything intolerable at that time.

9-FEMA management interviews at this time were saying no one properly estimated the scenario, and everyone was caught unawares. (WHAT!!!!!)

10-saw a news report in which a female representative of the black LA community blatantly suggested that if the area were white instead of mostly black, the response would have been different, faster..... (WHAT!!!)

11-evacuation from the Superdome to the Houston Astrodome commenced and completed on about day 5.

12-saw Oprah Winfrey's show taken into the area, between say day three and day five. This is the second time that there is an intimation that if the disaster had been in a white population area, the response would have been different. Also that the "situation" was a travesty. Not clearly stated as to what was the situation referred, and what was a travesty.

OK, with all that as a background, let's take a look again, and in addition I will add further information.

Start with the hurricane and all it's immediate damage as a natural catastrophe. Backing up some, there are several things to say about preparedness. In the preceding section I talked a bit about the fact that in the past, the capability was established by "proper resources", and let's say that if the decision was to build levees to a cat 3 hurricane, that is what was done, and everybody knew it. From there the responsibility to prepare for disaster is in the hands of many organizations; the mayor and New Orleans officials, the county officials, the governor and Louisiana officials, and lastly the Federal Government agencies, and the president. The president calls a "natural disaster area" and things are supposed to move from there through the natural machinations of government. All the way up the ladder, there was ample opportunity to look and assess, and act, if the parties had the inclination and the political sophistication to take action. On the city level there is absolutely no doubt that they had a very proprietary responsibility to insure the safety of the city. If for example, the subject of cat 3 vs. cat 5 levee capability was not discussed many times over many years, then shame. If it was discussed, did it move forward or fizzle? In the case of the city, there is also the issue of strength and repair of the levee system at any one time, such as yearly inspections, etc…, and was it in need of shoring up just due to age and disrepair? Next is the county, which could have joined political forces with the city; after all, New Orleans is a money maker and tourist attraction. We can't forget the state, and the issue with the state is that it could have and should have butted heads with the likes of Alaska on the building of an island bridge to serve a few thousand vs. upgrading the levee system in a city of millions, in some way. On the federal level, FEMA got folded into Homeland Security; note that the very word SECURITY means SAFETY. That means that the feds should use SAFETY as a key criteria in releasing federal funds, and it is up to the state to make the right case for SAFETY. It is up to the county and city to goose the state adequately.

So the hurricane came, and the levee broke. These events were out of the control of anyone at the immediate time frame at issue. So let's not overdo this portion of the issue. But now comes the real probe of significance. Where were the rescuers- city, county, state, federal, general citizenry? Did they take too long even given that the emergency conditions were extremely trying. Unless there is an emergency procedure already established, it would take time to assemble government response. I believe the general emergency procedure to a catastrophe is to put as many professional personnel into the area as warranted. Let's take the Sports Arena. At first, it must have seemed a godsend to have that much dry space available. However, without electricity, plumbing, food, it was a definite problem. Whether conditions or just bad organization prevented the entrance of support personnel, the Arena deteriorated into a disease and death trap. Liquids, solids, chemicals all contributed to an unhealthy atmosphere. And gangs- raping, shooting, killing, all contributed to chaos- how come???

I don't believe that any officials in any capacity could have deliberately slowed down the aid process. I can believe that if the city were a different one in a different location, it is possible that the city's own preparatory activity such as disaster planning, manpower, etc… might have been a little more appropriate. I think that is the planning that needed to be a city plan. I think that the magnitude of the disaster seriously cut down on the medical response capability, on the food and essentials distribution, on general disaster control.

I find it very hard to believe that on a state or national basis, the fact that New Orleans is over 70% black had anything to do with how the entire situation played out.

Today is the 7th of September, and the beginnings of some facts are coming out. The first is that the levee was not in disrepair, and that federal funds from as early as several years before this happened would not have been able to do much to the levee's anyhow.

Then comes an "as suspected", the mayor of New Orleans had over 200 school buses available to him before the storm actually hit. Each one could probably have handled over 100 people if you packed them in- he did not make them available. There was still time until just before the storm hit. Also, the plan was that the superdome would be used for evacuees, and the plan was a long-standing one. Where were the "port-a-potties", where was the food storage, the blankets, the flashlights, the generators, the other emergency items? Seems that the city and its officials (say the mayor for example) were totally inept. Now maybe they felt they would be embarrassed if the evacuation was not necessary, but to err the wrong way is inexcusable. That guy should be tossed to the dogs, instead of him railing at the state.

Seems also that a lot of people are wondering if Oprah jumped to conclusions too fast. Found out some interesting statistics. Several of the hardest hit areas were not in "Black Communities", but in the affluent white neighborhoods of neighboring states. Also that in Louisiana, over 70% of the damage was in "white areas", even though it is true that predominantly black New Orleans was badly hit. So the storm and the damage didn't give a damn if you were white or black, rich or poor, (just as I suspected).

Interesting and disappointing that President Bush took two days to make it to the scene, and then stayed a bit away from the action even when he was there. Interesting that Wal-Mart, the boon of the lower class, the antithesis of the upper class, began stocking shelves for the hurricane needs before the hurricane struck, and sent in millions of dollars of needed supplies immediately after the hurricane, using their own trucks. And FEMA officials initially turned the trucks away. I heard that the FEMA chief is a Bush/Republican appointee with actually no experience in this field. It surely seemed that way when he was interviewed. The man said on national TV that the FEMA never expected things to be so bad. What is he talking about? For days before the hurricane, it was being followed as a cat 5!!!!! How did he get into office, George? I am losing some respect for George the man as president, although if he was totally unaware and this is within the president's charter not to be aware of this level of appointee, then I retract my concern on this score. But the head of FEMA???? In the latest Brown development, not only did he get shunted out of direct disaster management, within a day after that, the man resigned. Seemed as if his resume included that he was a professor at a university (turns out he was a student), and that he was a manager of a "FEMA" type state organization (which it turns out he was not even employed there). My gosh, the nerve of this man to take the position, and the incompetence and absolute flagrant violation of every governmental protocol to place a neophyte, and a "truth stretcher" in this kind of position. And by the way, comes to light that three of Brown's underlings also had absolutely no experience in the field.

One of the things I fear is the uprising of a backlash to the perceived injustices to the affected people of the hurricane. I notice that the newspapers are beginning to show the devastation in areas other than New Orleans, and that is good, because the hurricane really didn't care who it was devastating, and hardly cared where it was doing the damage except by the low and high pressure regions that governed its movement.

Piece by piece the story is unfolding. The New Orleans mayor is culpable. The disaster planning document, funded by federal funds, clearly calls out evacuation, use of the Superdome for emergency, the feeding and provisioning for the housing of the people in the Superdome. The law is also quite clear. The first level of control is the city, the second the state, and Pres. Bush had called the Louisiana governor to ask if they wanted federal assistance. This is by law. The governor said NO. The governor's orders included turning away some

Wal-Mart trucks filled with supplies, and the turning away of the Red Cross with other supplies. So who is at fault????

Can't We All…..Along   Sept. 15, 2005

Watching the news, listening to Pres. Bush in New Orleans, in a scripted message to the world (actually to the people of the US, but of course, everyone can listen and see), I felt that the whole thing being dumped on him, and him accepting it, is incorrect and inaccurate. First, I think that each city and state has to have its own plan because they are the people who understand local conditions; second, since the law of the land says the federal govt. needs to ask if they are wanted, that put a valid constraint on the Feds. But you know what, I heard one "displacee" bitching and moaning "where was what he had been promised?" - that he had been "promised" a hotel room, a rent-a-car, a job on the docks. I don't think that he represents a large percentage of the people, but he is an ungrateful SOB to bash the system, and like persons likewise.

Bush said that the idea of the federal government stepping in sooner would be examined; I think that the House and Senate, representing State's Rights, will have an interesting task. It becomes apparent that a major disaster cannot be totally controlled and the recovery funded strictly by the locals, maybe even by the state, but between private enterprise nation-wide, and the federal government (perhaps oversight, perhaps a working part of the solution), it can be achieved.

Chapter 11-Some Things That Got Missed

Got an interesting awakening yesterday, from my daughters, and through my wife. I saw that being self-engrossed, even in the best of causes and interests, is sometimes offensive, sometimes too self-absorbing to the point where it is downright unendurable. All of a sudden, "The Four Agreements" basic tenets shouted out: Be true to your word, Make no Assumptions, Don't take things Personally, and Try your Best-they all found direct applicability.

Ever get so intensely engrossed in what you've got happening, that it takes on a life of its own? Well, this is what happened, and it involved small things that got blown up out of proportion. This is not to say that "small" is any less important than "large" in terms of events. Sure, some large things could mean "bang, you're dead". But guess what, when you screw up a little thing, it is relevant to you and your life style, and the people around you, and your emotional well-being.

So case in point, and extrapolate to yourself, and to any situation you want.

An epiphany: Time is a construct of man. Think about the fact that memory is a synonym for experiences, real or imagined. I am aware of events, people, things-that is my continuity, my existence and memory. Time is a chronology by definition-it moves as a tag. So what is real is experience, not a time-tagged moment.

November 2001: Flashback to when I retired. Today is eleven months after retirement, not a particularly important date in history, but one of relevance to me, and in my own opinion, a powerfully life-altering time shared with many people.

This relates to life style and change, and the interpersonal relationship between husband, wife, and children; and going beyond family, actually to friendships and acquaintances as well. I write this because the theme is universal, and the need to view the experiences may offer insights to others as they move forward into similar situations.

I believe I am a happy person, one who finds satisfaction in doing whatever occupies the day. That may sound like super-rationalization, however the reality of life is that meaning is achieved in the eye of the beholder, whether that beholder is self or whether the self feels others carry a loftier weight. There is the key to it all, in that if a person is comfortable with overall emotional, spiritual, and physical, surroundings, and projections of these, then more is really only a function of that person's perspective. Of course, there are shades to any simple statement, and so getting to the intellectual depth of the statements requires an expanded view.

And Another Thing

August 8, 2005: This one is far from easy. Driving this morning at 7:15AM on the 118- freeway to 5-freeway interchange, traffic was pretty much stopped. As I was just sitting there, waiting to move, I heard a slight thunk. When I looked to my right and a little behind me, I saw a motorcycle had just hit a wall; the front wheel was all wrapped around a body. The guy was in the middle of the whole motorcycle, his body looked too damn soft for him to still be alive. It was only a second, and it was a done deed. When I think about it, this guy got up in the morning, showered, shaved, dressed and whistled as he walked to his bike. And in less than two seconds he was snuffed.

October 8, 2005: Death again, but this time it's OK. Our Aussie (Australian Shepherd dog) was 14 years old, that's about 100, and we watched her go through the stages. In this case, it was a slow deterioration, and that is the nice thing about time, because both she and us got used to the gradual change, one that in this earthly body is an inevitability. This is where the moment and memory all play a part, because recall is the reality at this time. That includes when little Becky was a pup, as she grew and played, as she loved us and we loved her, as she became a mature little sweetheart. It's all there. Love her, and know that all is well for her.

One more: terrorism was the biggest thing on everyone's mind until Hurricane Katrina, and now for at least the near-term, the minds of most Americans are taken up with the consequences of the hurricane, not the least is the possible fomentation of a Racist overtone to the actions taken after the hurricane struck.

Again, I feel excited about writing all this stuff, because it is what is inside me. Sometimes, as I write, I think: "yeah", this is what is motivating, stimulating, exciting, and upsetting. It's good to channel concern into action, so long as the action isn't violent and disruptive or negative. Just a good shake-up. Of course, that's all relative, isn't it?

Sophistication is an interesting subject, especially when it is applied to anything worldly. For example, my daughter has a car with power windows. All of the actuators have failed at least once; the window regulator cable has failed on one door. As another example, this computer came with a wireless keyboard and mouse. In less than one month, the mouse batteries went belly-up. A friend of mine abandoned his brand new Cross Roller Pen when he found that the ink cartridges gave out very quickly, so he went back to ball-point pen.

I read a Science Fiction story about a general of a space fleet writing his memoirs. His side had massive overwhelming capability against the opposition, and then introduced one more level of sophistication, the ability to mass-transport in space. They lost the damn war because the transportation could not be suitably controlled to exact location. That one I stored away for a long time ago, and the former examples above just validate it. Far be it from me to nix progress, but every aspect needs to be assured before it's introduced. In System Engineering we look at COST, PERFORMANCE, SCHEDULE, SUPPORTABILITY, RISK (CPSSR) before we do the final decision-making. Where does this fit in the story being told here? Who knows, but it is interesting.

Part of it is the guerrilla tactics that go up against a full military force. There seems to be a place and use for each and every thing.

An Aside

June 21, 2005

You know, talking about all these really heady subjects, worrying about how to reshape the world so that it is a better place, sometimes we miss the local up-close-and-personal realities, whether good or bad. I just got kicked in the head with personal tragedy, my 95-year-old mother, who had a mastectomy at 85, had radiation treatment for a femur lesion at 94, and is now facing radiation again for a foot lesion at 95. Don't need to talk about fairness, because that it a relative thing and implies a plea to higher powers for relief, but the real message is that everywhere in the world people bear their own suffering, and don't need any help from outside to suffer more. So look at lofty goals that could be channeling support to betterment of the human condition, or at least, maintaining a laissez-faire attitude, instead of spearing everyone with the consequences of complaints of personal dissatisfaction.

I guess what is really going on in the terrorist realm is that the suffering produces mass hysteria on the part of some (or many), and creates psychoses that completely destroy any vestige of compassion and replace it with hatred. Nature sure does abhor a vacuum, so the method of tearing down to open a void and then filling it with the awful zeal of hatred is one that unfortunately works.

I have long noted that the new-borne babe is an open page upon which most anything can be written or impressed. Sure there is heredity as an aspect, and that defines scope, but not content. The content comes as acquired characteristics, provided by the environment, which includes all the minds and emotions with which the child comes in contact. And so what starts out as a straight arrow, standing upright and awaiting imprint, comes along as a result of the various pulls, pushes, bending, shaping, all in the name of education and conformance. No wonder everyone has baggage, I guess it's not really so bad, because one man's baggage is another's treasure. Besides, who's to judge?

This is where the concept of volitional science comes in. Here is a really interesting way to pull the personal inter-relationships into perspective. Believe in the concept of primary and secondary property: primary is the physical, secondary the mental/intellectual. Respect the sanctity of property and absolutely we can all get along. The "why" is because there is an underlying truth, and that is that man develops ego in order to survive in the physical world, the world of challenge to life, and so the ego is the cultivated weapon to protect the rest from annihilation. This is OK, because we are born into this physical world, and without developing protective mechanisms, we would have a problem surviving. Part of this rationale is that there is a cycle in process. The parents that nurture are also ego-carrying, and the development of ego is a flawed process, because although the ego develops responses to protect, it gets battered on the way.

Until or unless another basic mechanism comes into play, the best way to handle the flawed development of ego is to balance it with the best tools available. I think volitional science is one of these tools, and meditation is another. They are derived from different sources. Volitional Science is a method of allowing egos to co-exist without conflict. Meditation goes into and through ego and peels back the onion to reveal true nature. Both of these mechanisms are really tough to master, because they both need ego to eventually step aside. The problem is that our method of existence has placed ego at a very high level to insure continued existence. Circular logic, circular thinking, circular being.

But guess what, these things are not mutually exclusive. All of them are incremental, starting with ego-development as a separate path, then volitional science and/or meditation as re-directors. How a person balances these things is really their own call. How a culture or society imbeds these elements is really the critical thing. Here lies a hub, with spokes leading to annihilation or co-existence, but unfortunately, as we are seeing, nothing in-between. Scientific development that has placed widespread availability of deadly technology in the hands of warped personalities has created a precipice over which humanity can either jump or into which humanity will fall.

Managing change has always been the most critical aspect of any plan. This is true at this juncture as well. We cannot impose change without offering an acceptable transition plan. At this point, the plan has several alternatives, of which the paramount one is that if we do nothing; we stand the awe-full possibility of annihilation. I don't use this word indiscriminately; all the forces of destruction are clearly available in our wonderfully advanced technical environment. I see one of the many alternative plans in place at this time, but one severely flawed because it is limited to what I will call a "local" albeit very large problem, that of terrorists attempting to dismantle choices. A worldview is mandatory, not a fragmented approach with which so much of the world looks on and claims NIMBY.

Chapter 12-And What To Conclude About All These Things

Well, I've told my tale, and there are a lot of things that have bothered me, and a lot of offerings to resolve some of them. This is far from all there is, and the reason I stopped the issue parade is that "too much may just be too much". My objective was to get these things out on the table, off my chest, in your face, in plain view. My reason was that after talking to lots of people I came to realize that everyone had thoughts, but not everyone was doing something about them. Mobilization wasn't part of the plan, talking about it was. So here are a bunch of the things that hurt, and me having put them down, you can just ignore them if you wish, but the thoughts don't go away, they imprint and remain. So let me talk about some of the bottom lines on the various subjects, because that is how to get them going.

This stuff has been more than a simple ranting and raving. It has presented my personal point of view on many subjects; it has illustrated some of my own concerns in the world. It shows a level of paranoia, and I say I am proud of that, because that means deep involvement. No other way to really get anything started, talking about it without feeling it is just flat out cop-out. So a summary of the topics is in order.

First and foremost is saying hello to issues, recognizing that they are real, and that there are underlying things that foment these issues, and they cannot be denied. Second is to realize that many of these issues have common bonds, and therefore can be grouped, although not lumped. Third is that some of these common issues can be recognized as being amenable to the same solutions. Fourth is the realization that some issues run so deep that education, advertisement, propaganda, deprogramming, all methods of persuasion, may not be effective in modifying the mind of the individual.

Did you notice that throughout this missive, change and change control were subjects that kept on surfacing? It is the key to management, whether managing people, companies, things, your life. I am convinced that it is the way to a healthy social system, healthy financial system, and healthy personal life. It allows the past, present and future to all come together at once-you use your experience/memory today to see the continuum. Change is Zen Impermanence, a stalwart of Buddhist philosophy. There is a Zen saying that sits on my wall, it parallels the impermanence and change concepts:

"The past is the heart, the present the hand, the future the brain: all time is here.

All things perceived in the universe are within Mind,

All things in the universe are Mind."

I love it, because it shows the ability of man to flow. It is part of the summary of what needs to happen.

Man's own "inhumanity" is because of the lack of a way of properly dealing with himself, that is what "Volitional Science" can help resolve. It is a blueprint for interactions, and it lets each of us have a compassionate formula for interpersonal dealings. I say compassionate because it offers a fair bottom line basis for interactions. Put together these two concepts, and that is what this book has been all about, the interesting lack of application of these concepts has produced significant world dysfunction.

And I'd like to add a new thought, one I saw in a newspaper article by Thomas Friedman. He noted that crisis is a great catalytic opportunity, it knocks on the awareness of those it affects, and it offers leadership a unique opportunity to unite the citizenry to overcome the crisis. Well, we in the good old USA have had our fair share- we've had 9/11, we've had Katrina, we have illegal immigration, we have oil prices, we have impact of interest rates due to lack of understanding of basic personal finances, we have global warming, just to name a few. And each one is a lesson in economics and a potential lesson in leadership. I feel so bad, that these "Things of Concern", each a crisis with significant impact on my and your life, each an opportunity for leadership to step up and shine with well crafted future plans that look far ahead and say, "well, maybe not today, but in the planned and foreseeable future, we have a resolution happening", have all essentially stumbled, bumbled, and mumbled their way into the political, selfish self-interest categories. Do we know how to do anything right, anything well, anything timely? I am nervous that we are showing ourselves inept, and surprisingly, the consequence is that we are seen as inept, and respect has rightly dwindled.

But, it ain't over yet pal. We CAN correct our courses and we should do that. We owe it to ourselves, not to anyone else.

Chapter 13- And What Next?

You've read the book, and you may not agree with everything you have read. On the other hand, you may. Frankly, I expect that everyone will say "yea" to some items, and "BS" to others. So now comes choice, depending on your position. I really don't care what your position is, because if there is any inflammation as a result of reading, then I am happy. I did not want to convince you, I wanted to get you going. My style of writing is probably offensive, and even my opinions may be, but if you can get past the rhetoric, look at the issues themselves. And critically examine whether they are headed in the right direction (by the way, right is simply a matter of relativity, it could be left, or nadir, or zenith). But seriously, take a look and see if you are happy with things as they are progressing, if not, do something- something that means something to you personally. That is the difference. So here are some thoughts on what I would want to do, and darn it, I intend to get meaningful and do them.

First, I really feel strongly about Volitional Science and the concept of respect for the intellectual and physical property of others. I think the concepts should be part of school curricula, and start at a very early age, which I think means kindergarten. This will sensitize young people to what everyone has already had a taste of, the inequity of the bully, the concept of respect for others, the idea that what you do is what will move you along, and direction is of your choosing. This could continue and expand into course material that becomes increasingly sophisticated as the child becomes more capable of seeing a bigger picture. Andrew J. Galambos has written a very voluminous work on the subject. Lost track of it maybe 20 years ago, but it's around, and I think worth examining for content.

Hand in hand with Volitional Science is the idea of providing education to everyone. And I mean of a suitable quality of education so that combined with Volition, the product child walks out a thinking, caring, and aware human being, with hopefully a strong bent towards the concept of RESPECT.

Second, the threat of terrorism needs to be attacked on a world-wide basis. Read today that Russia and China are promoting that the UN modify its charter to be the unified "world-wide" anti-terrorism center of activity. Well done to these two as well as all the other countries supporting it. And perhaps set up the concept that if you don't lead, or follow, get out of the way. That means "taking the bull by the horns" and moving forward. It won't happen overnight, although "bull by the horns" implies that. There should be no retractions in this effort: once started, move forward, no backing up. It is too important to the future of humanity. The thing is that we need to converse in a positive manner, and to make headway. Committees are often laughed at because there are so many directions to take, each depending on the thought process of each committee member. So the standard approach needs to be taken. Set up the membership, set up the charter, establish the goals, delegate, and move forward. Don't just talk, act.

We need to step back and look at the functions of government, and on a world-wide basis. Forms of government need careful review, in terms of how they are performing, how imbedded in the cultures are they, can anything else be offered in the ensuing vacuum?

All these are interesting summaries of what to do next, but they lack depth, structure, and direction. That means where's the plan? So in the addendum to this missive, I have developed and present hopefully complete and independent plans for structure and resolution of what I will call "my" (meaning "our") issues.

Addendum-Offering Plans For Resolution

Introduction To Formulation

Everyone's got plans, that's the nature of the thinking man. But how are they structured, and do they follow through to implementation and maintenance? That is part of the difference between an idea and a reality, putting the thought to action. So I have put together my own outline of what a plan should/could consist of, then I have prepared offerings regarding each of the subject materials in this book, with each plan a separate entity. Lastly, after looking at all the potential solutions and plans, I have formulated a master plan that combines like-solutions, and hopefully presents an efficient, non-redundant structure to deal with as many of the issues as can be combined, and separate plans to deal with the others. I also have to say, that although I don't know this for sure, it appears that the surfacing programs may have a problem in that they tend to be a little constraining, maybe in the area of civil rights, and that is bad. So it may be that after these program-potentials surface, they will have to be modified or amended. Don't want, and can't have, a police state or anything like it-peace, respect, and freedom are the bywords, and they are obviously the antitheses of police state control.

One of the other things I have noticed is that as I formulated the action plans and then put a schedule to them, it forced me to focus intensely on the logic of the actions, the scope, and their viability. I have always felt that in the presentation of any action plan, the parameters of Cost, Performance, Schedule, Supportability, and Risk are essential parts of the material. They are obviously elements of any plan, but a presentation would be remiss if there is request for support, but no knowledge available as to scope of effort. However, I am in a quandary with respect to some of these parameters because the detail of activity is so immense that I feel that the capture of these aspects must be made after, rather than before the plans are drawn. So therefore, the budget, schedule, and maintenance support efforts can be placed into a mode of sustaining funding based on available funding at the onset, and then agreements as to how to infuse the support with both funding from the United Nations and separate funding from individual countries. You will also note that the plans presented do not go down to working level depth. They can't, because proper delegation requires that the participants be a major part of the preparation and the action. That also hampers my estimates of cost, which will really be quantified as the true scope of the various programs develops.

I have to say that venting my concerns was the easy part of this package, the toughest part is what follows, because it has to adequately address the issues, and present an embraceable set of solutions, in other words, "put my money where my mouth is". And, from my past experience in problem solving, one of the best parts of good solutions is simplicity, because if you build a house of cards, it WILL fall. So now comes as much time in the development of the solutions as I spent in the preparation of the material. And the thing of most concern to me is that given the seriousness of the material above, the shift in presentation for the resolutions is a dramatic change in perspective, from a literary presentation to a basic engineering-focused, problem-solving viewpoint. Whew!!!!!!!

I also need to make sure that what I pull together, no matter how logical it may be to me, does not become a ranting diatribe. Plus, certain things rang so true to me and appear so compelling in potential development of mind set, that I have ingrained them within the planning framework. So when you look and see such things as Volitional Science, and Capitalism, as inherent parts of programs, take another look at the earlier text for some of the presentation material that set the framework.

And lastly, although the things I say below are what I feel, and from my perspective, are both right and good, I have absolutely no doubt that many others will not agree. I think that is not only fine, but also exactly what I want; the dialogue about solutions is just as important as the solutions, because then everyone has ownership. BUT, dialogue is critical, and the most important part of it must be the firm and absolute goal of obtaining consensus and support for whatever plans ensue. AND they cannot be destructive in nature.

PROGRAM OUTLINE
(To be accomplished for each subject element)

(And at completion, to be melded with the other subject solutions)

Mission Statement: the overall reason for doing this, why this is important

Objectives: the goals to achieve

Values: the morals associated with the doing

Premises: givens at the time

Actions: implementation and assignment of responsibility, including the expectations of Cost, Performance, Schedule, Supportability, and Risk Assessment

SO HERE GOES

Global Terrorism

Mission Statement: To produce a civilization free from terrorist activity. There is a clear and present danger to the current status and even the existence of the (free) world, as well as to the continued existence of humanity, in the stated objectives of the Islamic terrorist organizations and their supporters. Their activities, which includes the threatening and taking of lives and the destruction of property, requires response through protection of innocents, possibly retaliation, perhaps in kind, and thus the consequence of potential escalation to an unacceptable level. There needs to be the obviation of that threat through the actions of all those threatened, and in a way that will preserve the freedoms of the free world and the lives and sanctity of its inhabitants.

Objectives: To contain, revolutionize, or eliminate. Through the combined actions of all those who perceive this as a threat, there will be established the methodologies of containment, re-education, and / or elimination of the terrorist perpetrators and their supporters. These three methodologies have an order and priority. Containment is first and most urgent, in that limiting terrorist influence will provide the opportunity to begin the decision process for implementing the other two. Containment can also mean isolation, which can be effective if there is suitable and mutual agreement of the protagonists. Re-education (or revolutionizing, turning around) is then the time-related second initiative, however, based on the intense psychological/religious propagandizing of the antagonists that may very well have taken place during early formative years, unless true re-orientation occurs there will be no recourse except the third alternative for those who refuse or cannot embrace the first two.

Values: Peace and freedom are the primary considerations. Protection of life and way of life are the primary sub-elements. That means not only of those being attacked, but a step back to look at these elements within the terrorist population as well. Every effort must be made to bring about a peaceful resolution in a peaceful way; however, terrorist tactics and those who perpetrate them must absolutely be eliminated as a method of human interchange. One key element is that we cannot substitute one issue for the other. Freedom remains an inherent part of the primary consideration.

Premises:

1. There is a hard-core terrorist element that will accept nothing but death as an alternative to failure in their cause.

2. This element will be accommodated if necessary.

3. Within the cadre of terrorists and terrorist supporters, there are those who can understand, and eventually truly concur that there are acceptable alternatives to the hard-core philosophy, this involving compromise and agreements.

4. A coalition dedicated to the elimination of this threat will receive worldwide acceptance and support, in civil, political, and military arenas.

5. Whatever solutions are under consideration, they will require adequate checks and balances to assure that the resulting societal definition maintains the values of peace and freedom.

Actions: In dealing with a worldwide threat of such horrendous potential consequences, it is necessary to establish a dedicated, efficient world-spanning effort. This will be an organization that will address all elements of response to threat, both short- and long-term. This organization will have three branches through which it will operate, the first being civil, the second diplomatic, the third being a military component. The plan is as follows:

6. Institute forum: Convene a world-level forum, with a mandate to review, develop, embellish, modify, and support this plan or its ensuing modification.

7. Develop action groups: Establish the multi-pronged organization, consisting of a civilian arm, a diplomatic arm, and a military arm. This organization will be focused in charter on the creation of conditions for, and then the

protection of, a peaceful and free humanity. Its funding will come from member nations, in proportion to national economic worth. This organization will be created and dedicated to the following:

a. Military- Develop a military branch: populated with dedicated multi-national peace-keeping and militarily-offensive personnel, the "Peacekeepers", drawn from member nations, <u>with a requirement to be allegiant to this organization while in service</u>, not to their originating nation. This will require complete support of member nations, and complete concurrence that any forms of action taken by this military will be swift, streamlined, and follow an absolute iron-clad charter with suitable checks and balances to assure that power is not usurped in any way. In order for this structure to be effective, there MUST be agreement from all supporting and contributing nations that their manpower will only be responsive to this organization. This arm will be observant of world conditions, working in concert with the diplomatic branch, and triggered to action through the diplomatic branches reactions to outbreaks of any violence or potential threats of violence. This organizational arm's first action against threat will be to immediately inform and consult with the diplomatic arm regarding pending responsive action. Policies and procedures previously developed will have had full concurrence from member nations, therefore minimizing response time to resolution. Time scale from decision for military action to actual action will not exceed 5 calendar days.

b. Diplomatic- Develop a diplomatic branch: populated proportionately with a cross-section of representatives of member nations, the make-up to be established by the organization. This arm consists exclusively of a diplomatic branch, whose purpose is to monitor status of peace, issue warnings as appropriate, convene immediate dialogue, issue sanctions and embargo if required, and to provide input and work in concert with the military arm as necessary. Time scale for each of these steps to be established, however, time period for each element will not exceed 15 calendar days.

c. Diplomatic-as a sub-set, no infringement on privacy: governance-develop suitable societal controls of government so that any introduced surveillance/monitoring technology can only be used within the universal adaptation of the values of peace and freedom.

d. Diplomatic- as a sub-set, prepare a civilian ISR (intelligence, surveillance, reconnaissance) capability: robotics/RPV's/satellites (with surveillance capability) to insure that areas covered have suitable observational data to provide real time protection, and to thwart the instigation of criminal acts. Although this may smack of a police state, in reality it provides one jump ahead of illicit action, and a careful population using such devices will have an overlying crime elimination methodology, rules governing use of the data to be determined by the activity above.

e. Diplomatic- as a sub-set, know with whom you are dealing: the development of an international identification for all persons, more robust than a driver's license or a passport. This document would include biological identifiers, and would require the receiver to insure suitable establishment of peaceful intent prior to issuance.

f. Diplomatic-as a SUPERSET, focus the United Nations organization on all forms of peaceful interaction: modification of the charter of the United Nations-this activity has the sole intent of placing the United Nations as a day to day operating body, not in any way related to the handling of war or peace. This body would deal with trade, with poverty, with education, and the like. However, it would clearly have as part of its charter the concept of a Polarization Decision: members are either for and support peace and freedom, or they are NOT. If not, they are not members, and will be dunned, expelled, and boycotted.

g. Diplomatic-as a sub-set, keep citizens informed of how and why their elected government is conducting its business: on a national basis, institute a "Decision Matrix Release", which provides all citizens with sufficient knowledge about decisions to provide confidence in leadership. This must include the facts that assure that any decision is safe and valid, and can tolerate the exposure to the population.

8. Establish a Civilian Support Arm-offer everyday involvement to the citizen:

a. Civilian- populated by everyday citizens. This effort to be associated with the concept of world-watch, which the intent of fostering a closer relationship between local neighborhood populations. Charter will be established at the national level of a country, with guidelines developed by the Diplomatic branch of the World organization. It is the charter of these civilian groups to thoroughly understand activity in their physical areas of responsibility, and to inform higher national levels of "untoward" activity.

b. Civilian-condemnation- [human actions are fueled by two drivers; external (such as an audience), and internal (raw emotion, powerful intellect…). The terrorists are no different. Ingrained is the internal aspect; hatred, thwarted desire, zeal. There is also an external component, this consisting of a seemingly "altruistic" desire to help the peer group, in this case, sympathizers and believers. Here the opportunity exists for the sympathizer community to re-examine any allegiance and determine if it is warranted. Turning that support around will cut off the external driver that activates the terrorist organization.] Muslim, Islamic, and any other communities that breed terrorist tendencies, need to refocus their priorities, allegiances, and interpretations. This means that the leaders of these communities can no longer preach and support the terrorist goals and activities. This means that the communities themselves need to condemn the acts of these groups. It starts with a ground swell of the community. That starts with the religious leaders turning the concepts around. [This will not be easy, because in fact, many of the leaders are fundamentalists in belief.]

c. Civilian-volunteer action- [as mentioned, there is a very large population of retired persons with extremely diverse backgrounds, and certainly high intelligence. It is time to put these people to volunteer work in two arenas.] The first action is the support and manning of any "World Watch" concept with the intent of identifying potential threat personnel. The second is the creation and dissemination of programs to re-educate people desiring to counteract the highly biased propaganda of certain religious training. Care must be taken to specialize the focus on the elimination of the fundamentalist actions that generate hatred and terror; therefore the material must be carefully reviewed by that religious hierarchy.

GLOBAL TERRORISM ORGANIZATION
"GTO"
PROGRAM IMPLEMENTATION SCHEDULE

7/20/2007

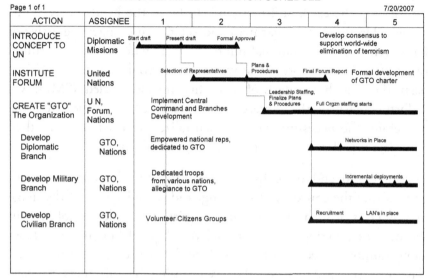

ACTION	ASSIGNEE	1	2	3	4	5
INTRODUCE CONCEPT TO UN	Diplomatic Missions	Start draft / Present draft / Formal Approval			Develop consensus to support world-wide elimination of terrorism	
INSTITUTE FORUM	United Nations		Selection of Representatives	Plans & Procedures	Final Forum Report	Formal development of GTO charter
CREATE "GTO" The Organization	U N, Forum, Nations		Implement Central Command and Branches Development	Leadership Staffing, Finalize Plans & Procedures	Full Orgzn staffing starts	
Develop Diplomatic Branch	GTO, Nations		Empowered national reps, dedicated to GTO			Networks in Place
Develop Military Branch	GTO, Nations		Dedicated troops from various nations, allegiance to GTO			Incremental deployments
Develop Civilian Branch	GTO, Nations		Volunteer Citizens Groups		Recruitment	LAN's in place

WMD

Mission Statement: We cannot allow consequential weaponry that can destroy the earth and mankind, to be in the hands of irrational beings. Until the time that mankind is either no longer aggressive or has developed a fully rational mind-set, there will remain the realities of efforts to protect a society as well as efforts to dominate it. On this basis, the most horrendous of weaponry, the class called WMD, will unfortunately be in the minds of the aggressors as well as the defenders. Therefore, the necessity exists to neutralize the need for, and then eliminate this class of, as well as all, weapons of war.

Objectives: An end to the threat of use of WMD. The consideration of neutralizing the concepts, stockpiling, and consideration of the usage of WMD, is of such import that it requires a complete revolution in the ways of thinking of the inter-relationships of humankind. Laws alone cannot protect, because the "Law" has been the result of the "law-breaker" in order for the law-forming organizations to have come into existence and to impose penalties. Mankind cannot wait for the threat to manifest, rather an active plan must be instituted to prevent the inception of such programs. Herein lies the magnificence of mankind, in that the young mind can be educated and brought to a state of knowledge. Thus, the highest level of response to such a mission statement is that of teaching our youth to respect life and the concepts of free will and free choice. The objectives are to:

1. Develop a world level organization to monitor and thwart the development of such weaponry. There will be three schools of thought on this; one being that no such technology should be developed, a second being that technology can be controlled and therefore proper monitoring is adequate, and the third that certain organizations must be the repositors and controllers of such weaponry and technology.

2. Develop a world level organization dedicated to the elimination of the current expansive existence of such weaponry.

3. Institute the ideas of Volitional Science, guiding the mind toward the loftier goals of recognition of self-worth and recognition and respect for both physical and intellectual property.

Values:

The entire consideration is the protection of the existence of life on this planet of ours. Care is essential to insure that what we have does not get either polluted or destroyed. Life is precious, and peace is a requisite to quality of life. Once life is protected and assured, and peace is established, then freedom will be a natural outgrowth, and fear will be eradicated.

Premises:

1. A world-view is essential, implying that all nations provide full support to the concepts of elimination of WMD as a threat to mankind.

2. Funding for monitoring organizations will be drawn from a dedicated account populated with levied funding from all nations, proportional to GNP.

3. Each country will support the concepts of universal education.

Actions:

1. Institute forum and define group structure: Convene world-level meetings, with mandate to review, develop, and create the organizations necessary to satisfy the charter. Define an over-viewing organization with two branches, one with monitoring capability, the second with response capability. The overview group is to consist of select individuals with no allegiance to nation, but to a universal consideration of mankind. The over-view group will synthesize any monitoring status with the need for actions, and will authorize such action if required.

2. Develop Action Branch-Monitoring: Create an international organization with monitoring jurisdiction. This authority shall contain the ability through diplomatic contact, scientific contact, and scientific instrumentation, to monitor the status of research and production of the

elements that contribute to illicit development of WMD. The action of this organization will be the reporting of status to an over-viewing body. The organization is to be permanently staffed by personnel drawn from the various nations.

3. Develop Action Branch-Response: Create an organization with the charter to eliminate offending activities that support the concepts of WMD. This organization will receive its assignments from the over-viewing body.

4. Provide Curricula of Education (of the young towards developing respect for all.) All countries and their citizens will contribute to and be part of a world-wide educational effort to introduce the larger perspective of individual freedom of thought and action, given that there is no harm to others from the actions that ensue. The key will be the creation of a world-level system with uniform standards and uniform curriculum for use in all schooling, as well as local material related to the needs of the community. It becomes essential that nationalistic interests be melded within the overview, and that well-crafted integration with the needs of nations and locales be developed.

Recognizing that the specific focus of this initiative is WMD, then a rational appreciation of the potential catastrophic impacts and consequences of the existence of this weaponry must be deeply impressed on all. The general populace must recognize that leadership representatives must have a dedicated agenda to the containment and elimination of WMD.

WMD ORGANIZATION
"WMDO"
PROGRAM IMPLEMENTATION SCHEDULE

7/20/2007

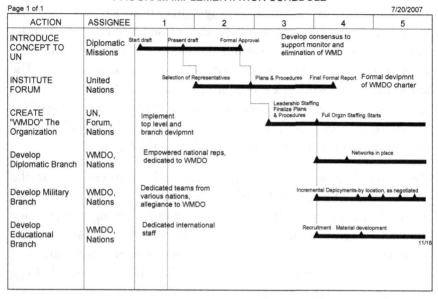

ACTION	ASSIGNEE	1	2	3	4	5
INTRODUCE CONCEPT TO UN	Diplomatic Missions	Start draft Present draft Formal Approval		Develop consensus to support monitor and elimination of WMD		
INSTITUTE FORUM	United Nations		Selection of Representatives	Plans & Procedures Final Formal Report	Formal devlpmnt of WMDO charter	
CREATE "WMDO" The Organization	UN, Forum, Nations	Implement top level and branch devlpmnt		Leadership Staffing Finalize Plans & Procedures Full Orgzn Staffing Starts		
Develop Diplomatic Branch	WMDO, Nations	Empowered national reps, dedicated to WMDO			Networks in place	
Develop Military Branch	WMDO, Nations	Dedicated teams from various nations, allegiance to WMDO		Incremental Deployments-by location, as negotiated		
Develop Educational Branch	WMDO, Nations	Dedicated international staff		Recruitment Material development		11/18

THE ECONOMY

Mission Statement: The development of a world-level economy: World level population is viewed as a <u>geographic</u> construct, that view has been instrumental in the development of sociological communities and corresponding sociological differentiation. Thus, economies have developed along artificially created geographical separations. The introduction of a world-view economic system would raise the levels of economic existence of all nations. This international inter-twining of the cultures, the societies, the morals, of all the various cultures, will promote the development of a single world population, the human race.

Objectives: Increase world level affluence: It is intended that the establishment of true world markets allowing and promoting open and free trade with all participants, will result in increasing affluence for all, availability of resources to all, sharing of technological advances; blending of cultural lines as economic lines of demarcation dissolve, and tolerance as people find they mutually benefit in their dealings with each other. The mechanism for this development is the universal spread of capitalism.

Values: To share through availability: the universal non-discriminator- the vending machine: the world becomes the customer, with products available to <u>all</u>. To be accomplished with respect.

Premises:

1. The selfishness of individuals within humanity and the desire to increase personal wealth are an integral part of this process. Insuring respect and Volitional Science's regard for property are the prerequisites to achieving these goals.

2. Education will be provided to all nations' populations. The development of the educational programs curricula must be coordinated with all groups.

3. A thorough review of assets, attributes, resources, will be accomplished at national levels, to allow the identification

of the major contributions to the world economy that can be made by the various geographically established nation-states. Centers of Excellence will naturally come forth.

Actions:

1. Institute forum: Convene a world-level forum, with a mandate to review, embellish, modify, and support this plan or its ensuing modifications. Representation from each and every country is essential.

2. Develop Action Groups: Establish expertise, consisting of economics experts from various nations, to develop a system and plan for the creation of a world economy.

   a. Promote the creation of the educational system adjunct which will propagate the concepts of volitional science, property, capitalism, and a universal morality

   b. Develop the plan to identify attributes of nation-states, perform cost-benefit analyses to determine where development of resources is to take place, how best to provide the products to the market place

   c. Review the concepts of either totalitarianism, socialism or capitalism utilized within an area to determine the applicability of change to produce the best societal aspects for each culture.

   d. Establish research and development initiatives to explore and support energy alternates

   e. Develop a long-range plan for the development of national industries, for the eventual elimination of the tariff concept.

   f. Develop world-level communications capabilities.

3. Prepare the Organization: Establish world level economic guidelines for capitalism, the social system based on recognition of individual rights (including property rights).

4. Implement the Organization: Establishment of World level government, where such government will be solely for the purpose of protecting the rights (man's freedom of action in a social context, the right to life and property) of its citizenry.

THE ECONOMY
WORLD LEVEL
PROGRAM IMPLEMENTATION SCHEDULE

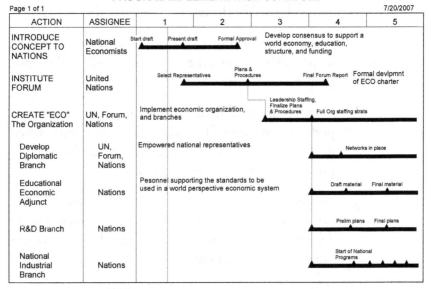

ACTION	ASSIGNEE	1	2	3	4	5
INTRODUCE CONCEPT TO NATIONS	National Economists	Start draft	Present draft	Formal Approval	Develop consensus to support a world economy, education, structure, and funding	
INSTITUTE FORUM	United Nations		Select Representatives	Plans & Procedures	Final Forum Report	Formal devlpmnt of ECO charter
CREATE "ECO" The Organization	UN, Forum, Nations	Implement economic organization, and branches		Leadership Staffing, Finalize Plans & Procedures	Full Org staffing strats	
Develop Diplomatic Branch	UN, Forum, Nations	Empowered national representatives			Networks in place	
Educational Economic Adjunct	Nations	Personnel supporting the standards to be used in a world perspective economic system			Draft material	Final material
R&D Branch	Nations				Prelim plans	Final plans
National Industrial Branch	Nations				Start of National Programs	

ILLEGAL IMMIGRATION (anywhere)

Mission Statement: To respect the respective policies of a country: The open flow of people between borders should be a positive sign of world-view. However, it is inappropriate and a flagrant violation of national prerogative to consider non-citizens as anything but transients with special dispensation associated with government-sponsored temporary status. How national prerogative includes controlling entrance of non-citizens, and controlling the issuance of immigration papers, is specifically the charter of the respective government. Illegal immigration (which really means difference from national rules, as well as sneaking in with intent to stay) imposes burden on citizens, cannot be condoned, and must be stopped.

Objectives: To identify and rectify the current status of non-legal individuals, and to develop proper controls:

1. To enforce current laws that prohibit the flow of illegal immigration into a country. (This by the way is redundant.)

2. To review the current laws for decision on whether they are adequate and to consider revision to such laws regarding the scope of their jurisdiction.

3. To initiate legal review to determine better definition of "illegal immigrant" and status thereof, review the process of granting citizenship, review the benefits made available to illegal immigrants.

4. To institute actions commensurate with the conclusions and modifications per above.

Values: Insure a smooth transition: The systems allowing immigration into this or any country were designed with procedures to allow determination and control of the number of entrants. Unless and until this system is modified, it stands as the law of the land. Advantage may not be taken by circumventing the process and its limits. Persons here illegally must be brought into accountability, and segued into either an acceptance program (if one exists or is created) or returned to their origins. Respect for those hard-working persons here now must also acknowledge their illegal status and initiate a process to either create a path to legality of status, or to initiate deportation. Such items as health care and welfare will be treated as transition items for illegal immigrants. This means that after a specified period of use, the support will be withdrawn. The values are in place to honor citizens and to minimize impact on those here illegally, but nonetheless, to reconcile the problem.

Premises:

1. It is wrong to be here illegally.

2. Legislation begins with acknowledging the rules as they exist today.

3. A man's needs are not a requirement on another mans life.

4. So long as the legal system (created by law through the legal decisions of the population) will condone something, it is acceptable.

Actions:

1. All actions are government related, since the entire immigration process is the interaction between individuals and a country, and the government is the elected representation for protection of the citizenry. (After all, the purpose of government is to protect its citizenry, redundantly stated, but essential to stress). This means that the laws need review and enforcement.

2. The first move is the consideration of cause. Immigration is from someplace, to someplace. The reasons for leaving, although varied, all relate to a desire to depart and a desire to arrive. Therefore the first but recognizably one of the toughest actions is a review of the sources of the illegal immigrants, and a dialogue with the home country to understand and possibly modify some of the causes of exit.

A State Department charter will be initiated to undertake this dialogue, with two underlying themes- the first to eliminate obviously correctable causes of departure, the second to require the acceptance of the returned illegal immigrants to their mother country, and appropriate actions undertaken. In the event that an illegal is tied into a minor violation within the country, warning will be given, and a time period allocated for correction. A second such violation makes the time period immediate and converts to a major violation . A major violation triggers immediate return to the mother nation. This concept applies to any services provided to a person here illegally, such a person or family will receive the one time service, but not a second time. In summary, at the uncovering of the condition, there is a transition time to allow a person to correct conditions or leave, however, if and when there is a second action, the response will be "two strikes and you are out, now".

3. Establish tighter border control, with the consequences to offenders being financial, and including physical labor as a barter to handle fines. Maybe them apples will help people see the light that something for nothing just isn't a good thing for ALL the involved people. This concept of something for nothing IS the source of concern at the receiving nation, since due process would allow immigration according to a set standard, including a fixed number of persons.

4. To review the immigration laws, and to insure that the concept of sponsors is in place, with the intent of assuring that each and every applicant has a means of gainful employment and a method of integrating into the society.

Joseph K. Goldstein

IMMIGRATION PROGRAM
INS
PROGRAM IMPLEMENTATION SCHEDULE

4/28/2006

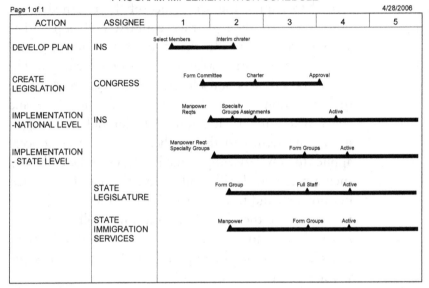

ACTION	ASSIGNEE	1	2	3	4	5
DEVELOP PLAN	INS	Select Members	Interim chrater			
CREATE LEGISLATION	CONGRESS	Form Committee	Charter		Approval	
IMPLEMENTATION -NATIONAL LEVEL	INS	Manpower Reqts	Specialty Groups Assignments		Active	
IMPLEMENTATION - STATE LEVEL		Manpower Reqt Specialty Groups		Form Groups	Active	
	STATE LEGISLATURE		Form Group	Full Staff	Active	
	STATE IMMIGRATION SERVICES		Manpower	Form Groups	Active	

EDUCATION, and VOLITIONAL SCIENCE

Mission Statement: Prepare young people early, for society, civilization, and self-sufficiency by giving them the best available thinking tools: The human condition starts with only one instinct, that of suckling. That instinct insures immediate survival, if there is sustenance to be had for the infant. Beyond that one instinct, the human must learn everything else: rudimentary hunting skills, reactions to the environment, inter-action with others.... Thus, in human society, education is absolutely critical to the well being of the growing child. It becomes the goal of an <u>unbiased</u> educational system to assure a balanced learning experience, one that provides the skills of physical survival, the ability to think and react clearly, to interact with others and the environment, and to make the most of the human capability. All people should have the availability to such an education.

Objectives: Develop programs geared to a population's societal requirements: Equality of opportunity to exposure to the various processes, procedures, and materials to insure availability- universal availability of education. The process includes standard technical subjects geared to the ability of the recipient, such as reading, writing, arithmetic, and rudimentary science; emotional development; volitional science. To establish a universal program that allows the selection of volitional science and capitalism theory and practice as part of the educational system.

Values: Each and every human involved within civilization must be recognized as to their capability to exist within, and to contribute to, humanity as developed through the process of living.

Premises:

1. Universal standards will be implemented.

2. All people will be eligible.

Actions:

1. Development of International Education Standards, to provide both suitable materials and adequate, unbiased depth of

coverage. One overall administrative body will be created to oversee local shaping and development of curriculum. This management body will be staffed by an internationally selected group of educational leaders. Beneath this governing body will be staffs whose functions DO NOT relate to nations, but to an international prospectus, as delineated below.

2. Assurance of availability of education. All countries to subscribe to this program, and to have the flexibility to adjust curriculum and methodologies but within the boundaries of the program.

3. Creation of standards for certifying the teaching skills. Initial staff to be trained by teams from the management body, and then distributed within the existing school staffs as the school staffs are brought up to standards.

4. Introduction of meditation as a portion of the education curriculum. Here is one example where education will receive a rounding out to include things beyond the 3 R's.

5. Introduction of volitional science as a portion of the educational curriculum. Here again, the concepts of education will be expanded to promote development of strong social and societal norms.

6. Introduction of capitalism as one choice of societal method of economy. This does not preclude other choices.

UNIVERSAL EDUCATION
PROGRAM IMPLEMENTATION SCHEDULE

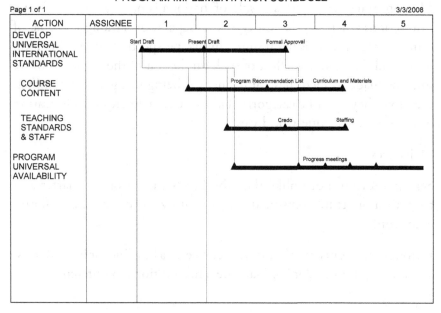

Global Conflict

Mission Statement: As a result of nationalism, and its correlating distinctions, there are large degrees of separation amongst people of different regions. This has resulted in two perspectives, one being local needs and the other the effect of such on the rest of the world. A move must be made to shed these differences as being instigators of conflict, therefore they must be categorized as cause to help create a unification of ideas towards a one-world view.

Objectives:

Set up a forum, not unlike the UN, but with a stronger charter and teeth to support it, to insure dialogue that by its very nature, will pre-empt conflict.

Introduce the concept of volitional science, as a baseline for interactions, as a method for developing dialogue, and solutions to differences.

Values:

Nothing is more important than developing the baselines of understanding between peoples, and this means RESPECT.

Premises:

1. All nations want to prevent expensive and life-threatening conflict.

2. All nations would rather obtain their ways through peaceful means than by warfare and/or loss of life.

3. Those not supporting the above must change or be changed, this in the interest of self-preservation of humanity.

Actions:

1. Establish an organization that will produce a universal educational system insuring the inculcation of the concepts of volitional science.

2. Establish a committee to draft and propose a charter for

the acceptance by all nations of the concepts of volitional science within the rules of governance of the nation.

3. Populate the committee with empowered members of each nation, to create the charters for the adaptation of the science within the countries constitution, and then the implementation within the member nation

4. Establish a forum organization, which will insure platform for meaningful dialogue regarding issues of a global nature.

5. Establish a capitalistic world-level economy, which by nature, will interlink all participants.

GLOBAL CONFLICT RESOLUTION
"GCR"
PROGRAM IMPLEMENTATION SCHEDULE

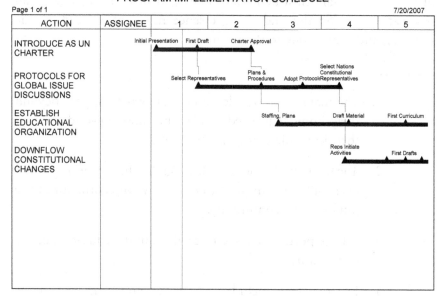

ACTION	ASSIGNEE	1	2	3	4	5
INTRODUCE AS UN CHARTER		Initial Presentation / First Draft	Charter Approval			
PROTOCOLS FOR GLOBAL ISSUE DISCUSSIONS		Select Representatives	Plans & Procedures	Adopt Protocols	Select Nations Constitutional Representatives	
ESTABLISH EDUCATIONAL ORGANIZATION				Staffing, Plans	Draft Material	First Curriculum
DOWNFLOW CONSTITUTIONAL CHANGES					Reps Initiate Activities	First Drafts

Page 1 of 1   7/20/2007

The Environment

Mission Statement: Provide a highest quality of life environmental baseline: Man is the only creature that shapes his environment in such a world-influencing manner. The environment of the planet and therefore of man's surroundings must be thoughtfully and carefully considered in each and every decision by which it is affected.

Objectives: No pollution and no destruction: In consideration of the egocentric nature of man, it is essential to ensure the continued existence of man by safeguarding the environment in which man exists, especially against himself. The balance of nature must be insured, the purity of the atmosphere must be protected, the detrimental effects of man's usage of the resources of the world must be eliminated, and the effects of man's existence should be that of improvement.

Values: Although the word "Nature" is an all-inclusive implication that there is such a being, in reality it represents the entire physical system of the world. Man must be harmonious with this system, since Man is a part of it. So the underlying essence must softly tread on the territory, and cannot offend the future.

Premises:

1. The majority of people do not care what happens beyond their immediate needs, or at the most, beyond their or their immediate progeny's lifetimes.

2. The cost of the policy, although it should be measured over millennia, must not be offensive or exorbitant in the minds of the community.

3. A large portion of the effort will be in the educating of the community.

4. Environment includes air, land, and sea, as well as occupants thereof.

Actions:

1. First and foremost is the need for recognition as a problem. This is a sensitivity analysis that needs to be imposed over the structure of man's viewpoint of himself. Each and every human being forms a relationship with the environment, and the key is to upgrade the priority of that relationship with the physical environment. A prioritizing of the essentials within Maslow's list is an essential ingredient.

2. Since energy and energy production are such large portions of the impact on the environment, a matrix of alternative energy sources needs to be prepared, developed, presented and selected to the appropriate decision makers. A technical board will be developed and staffed to prepare such recommended alternatives.

3. Private industry must contribute to, and be a part of the oversight necessary to implement and enforce policy. An Environmental Policy Board will be formed, with world-level jurisdiction.

4. Private industry must be factored into the environmental costs and penalties of the decisions. Suitable jurisdictional laws, policies, procedures, and impact assessments will be developed.

5. Education is to be expanded to include appreciation, recognition, and accountability of the impact of human civilization on the world environment.

Joseph K. Goldstein

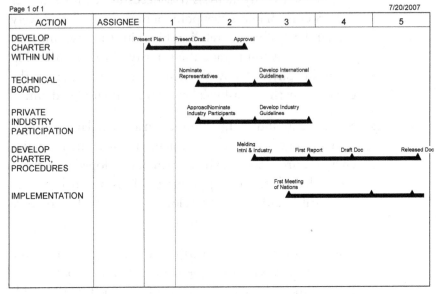

ENVIRONMENTAL PROTECTION
"EP"
PROGRAM IMPLEMENTATION SCHEDULE

Page 1 of 1   7/20/2007

ACTION	ASSIGNEE	1	2	3	4	5
DEVELOP CHARTER WITHIN UN		Present Plan · Present Draft · Approval				
TECHNICAL BOARD			Nominate Representatives	Develop International Guidelines		
PRIVATE INDUSTRY PARTICIPATION			ApproaclNominate Industry Participants	Develop Industry Guidelines		
DEVELOP CHARTER, PROCEDURES				Melding Intnl & Industry · First Report	Draft Doc	Released Doc
IMPLEMENTATION				Frst Meeting of Nations		

Drugs

Mission Statement: Elimination of the deleterious and addictive: The effect of the cultivation, production, and distribution of illegal, detrimental drugs and products is a major drain on economies and people. First is the requirement to examine the illegality and place universal standards on that designation. A need exists to curtail first and then eliminate such infrastructure as produces such products for availability to the general population, and to allow societies and their occupants to recover from the deleterious effects of this sub-culture.

Objectives:

1. Redirect the resources from punitive involvement against the drug trafficking trade, into positively productive effort.

2. Eliminate the dependency on the products, physically, financially, and psychologically. This includes not only those who use the product, but also those who are involved in producing it.

3. Develop a societal recognition of set and setting, to thus redirect the energy of illegality to a socially acceptable system. (This does not imply wanton abandon, rather judicious use associated with new standards and mores).

Values:

Lives can be focused away from underground anti-societal activity. Once again, gradual change will be introduced for those dependent, but as abrupt as necessary for those trafficking. Set and setting will be discussed, developed, and incorporated into society.

Premises:

A large international support system will be available

Actions:

1. Education of the young is essential. This will start through

the educational programs to be established by a world-organization that will include all educational basics as part of a universal program, and locale specific education related to country, nationality, locale.

2. A break in the chain of neighborhood familiarity. In areas where current drug culture is ingrained into the society, a specialized and focused set of experiences will be placed within the teaching curriculum.

3. Teeth will be applied to actions. After establishing the laws within the society, enforcement of these laws will commence with first eradication of the source material, then capture and corrective action towards the personnel involved.

4. International laws will be created and enforced. The creation will build on the already existing system, but will work through the requirements flow-down process to the local level.

5. A set of programs established to divert the efforts of growers, manufacturers, distillers, distributors, to other efforts that can use their expertise channeled into acceptable societal endeavors.

6. Convene international forum to develop long-term plans to establish set and setting for the concepts of addicting elements, for the concepts of religious elements, and for recreational elements.

DRUG CONTROL
"DCP"
PROGRAM IMPLEMENTATION SCHEDULE

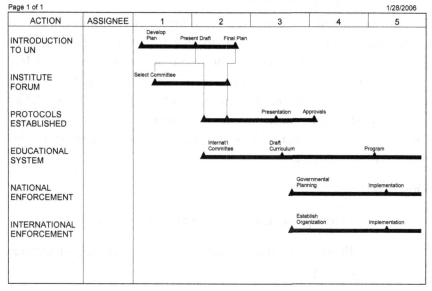

ACTION	ASSIGNEE	1	2	3	4	5
INTRODUCTION TO UN		Develop Plan — Present Draft — Final Plan				
INSTITUTE FORUM		Select Committee				
PROTOCOLS ESTABLISHED				Presentation — Approvals		
EDUCATIONAL SYSTEM			Internat'l Committee	Draft Curriculum		Program
NATIONAL ENFORCEMENT				Governmental Planning		Implementation
INTERNATIONAL ENFORCEMENT				Establish Organization		Implementation

Joseph K. Goldstein

HURRICANE AT LARGE-Response to Natural Disaster

Mission Statement: It is the responsibility of elected government to insure and provide many things, in this instance, methodology to generate safety and recovery in the event of catastrophe. In a free society, there is no "right to be protected against catastrophe", merely the freedom to subscribe to protection, which should be made available. Herein lies the charter line, to offer the probability of protection, and the services that are consequent to a disaster. The availability of this charter must be insured.

Objectives:

1. Develop the mechanism to offer the services required

2. Provide adequate fore-warning of pending disastrous consequences.

3. Support the plans necessary to provide safe haven, or suitable methods of repair and protection, during any situation.

4. Establish a hierarchy of response and responsibility.

5. Respond to disaster.

Values:

The charter of election includes the subsequent delegation of responsibility by the elected, for citizen safety where such purview is beyond the ability of the individual.

Premises:

1. The society can be educated to recognize the benefits of such service insurance.

2. Private industry can become a supplier as necessary to a government overview.

3. The transition from local to national to world-level response can be diplomatically established.

Actions:

1. Establish private industry and government representation to participate in creating the concepts and development plans for a private industry approach to disaster awareness, preparation, and response.

2. Review and propose modification and transition from existing definitions of responsibility.

3. Establish the mechanisms that will transition from government responsibility to the free enterprise arena.

4. Coordinate local, county, state, federal charters, to be immersed within the private industry developments.

5. Prepare and /or review/amend disaster plans

6. Revise charters, redefine responsibility as required

7. Initiate multi-year plan reviews and status of actions.

Joseph K. Goldstein

HURRICANE/NATURAL DISASTER
"NATDIS'
PROGRAM IMPLEMENTATION SCHEDULE

7/20/2007

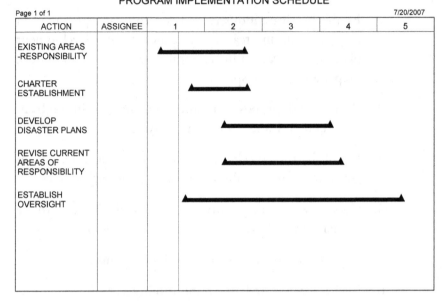

ACTION	ASSIGNEE	1	2	3	4	5
EXISTING AREAS -RESPONSIBILITY						
CHARTER ESTABLISHMENT						
DEVELOP DISASTER PLANS						
REVISE CURRENT AREAS OF RESPONSIBILITY						
ESTABLISH OVERSIGHT						

Pregnancy, Birth, Old Age, And Death

I always thought that education would be the correct answer to all our social problems. I still say that education could do it, but it isn't obvious that education will reach everyone. But the consequences of poor personal planning are felt by the whole society, because guess who pays? So the problem just got passed like a buck, and to all of the minions of society.

I realize that this section is somewhat different than the others, in that it looks more at the generic nature of living, and not at specific societal problems, although who says that these subjects are not societal issues? But I will treat them as I have treated the other sections, and offer input as to methods of addressing these items.

Mission Statement: propose societal mores that most effectively handle issues associated with pregnancy, birth, old age, and death. Since each of these conditions is a normal part of living, the essential aspect is to minimize any awkwardness of experiencing them. This means that as each of us experience these living conditions, they should not create trauma in our lives, but rather a sense of expectation and comfort in dealing with them.

Objective: Establish educational and institutional level programs that generate careful planning on the part of citizenry to produce an individual path that comfortably deals with each aspect of life. It would appear that reaching each of these phases of life is the easy part, and that suitable accommodation is the tough part of implementation.

Values: Respect is the key aspect. At the core is the experience of the "experience". This means that the subject must be satisfied with the condition. Second is the respect by the "experience-ee's" community. This means that all who touch the life of a person must have regard for that person's condition. Third is the respect for choice. This is of each and everyone involved, and the ability to say yes, no, or be indifferent.

Premises:

1. There is no time limit towards the resolution of this agenda

2. A correlation between religious belief and the establishment of this program is essential.

Actions:

1. Create panel to define the scope of the program-national/international, religious scope, sociological implications, educational impacts, panel makeup. This is the key part, wherein it becomes essential to have representation from all existing societies, with all the various needs and conditions clearly to be recognized and to have personnel who can address all the issues and possibilities. In addition to program scope, it is necessary to layout the program guidelines, to be disseminated to the various sociological and geographical areas to create their own operating programs, those which will be used to address issues relating to the four key items. It is expected that many cultures will have satisfactory perspectives today, and therefore complete change is not required. Only when the guidelines provided are in conflict with the societal mores will it become necessary to develop suitable change.

2. Develop plan to initiate program. Once the various societies have responded with recommended modifications to their own cultures will the program then escalate to the next level wherein program initiation will be instituted. The disparatity between current and future styles will determine the extent and timing of the initiation of change. This will also include the consideration of type of program staffing.

3. Staff program. This aspect will involve both indigenous and external staffing. Care must be taken to insure that the mix of personnel assures fair and valid voices as the detail of the program is developed.

4. Present draft-This is the effort to insure that the program truly represents the needs and desires of the effected peoples. Here a suitable committee, consisting of management staff, working staff, guest experts, will review the program plan and the specific details to insure that implementation is a positive action.

5. Institute program

PREGNANCY, BIRTH, OLD AGE, AND DEATH
PROGRAM IMPLEMENTATION SCHEDULE

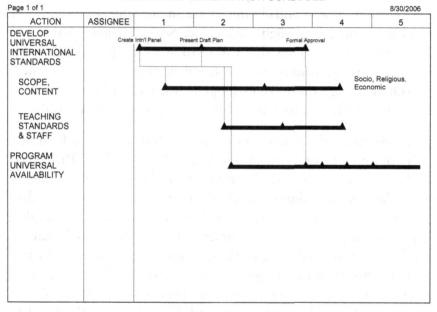

Chapter Last-The Royal Combination Of Programs

What I have done so far is prepare a series of independent programs based on the chapters within this document. These are surely areas of concern, and each schedule can stand alone, although some slight poetic license has been taken in the time spans of events. I had an ulterior motive, and that was to try and line up some of these programs (where it made sense) according to the action steps within each. Where I found that some essentially mirror the implementation of others, I think combining them might make sense. So this section is that logical combination of programs that will provide a synergy and significant savings in management activity, cost, and effort in the long-run. There remains the danger that too big a program will never make it, and in that event, the breakdown back to individual programs is still available.

As I considered which programs grouped well together, I realized that they fell into a natural pattern of division: "The World as Threatened by Utter Destruction", "The World in the Fight Against Conditions", and "The Nation Within Its Borders". There are some areas that relate specifically to various nations themselves. I believe, in this case, that confining my activity and recommendations to the United States is the best way to handle these subjects, since each country is in fact an independent entity and political body, and would deal with these internal subjects as their laws, cultures, and mores dictate. Those subjects are ILLEGAL IMMIGRATION, and NATIONAL DISASTERS. Thus, there can be two overall programs set up with internal detailing covering the specifics.

For the programs dealing with the UNITED NATIONS subjects, as I looked at the program implementation schedules, I saw that the United Nations was called upon frequently as the starting point for kickoffs of many of the programs. That made me realize that perhaps a restructuring of the United Nations, to incorporate the necessary functions of the programs, might in fact be an acceptable method for managing all the elements of the programs. Hopefully, it should be easiest to build on an existing infrastructure than to create a new one. There may, however, be resistance to change in the status quo, as well as the resistance to new concepts and authorities. I would expect a certain amount of reticence towards dismantling, modifying, or building a parallel structure that lessens the existing functions. Oh boy, looks like a big bite to chew no matter which way it goes. Focusing on modifying the existing functionality seems to me to be the best way, because in reality it should satisfy those concerned, since it will increase the tasking of the overall organization and provide both increased meaning to its existence, and increased purpose to its function.

The United Nations has involvement and action in many of the areas of concern, however, the current timetables of the UN as an organization are long-term, and many of their actions are limited by current charter. This is understandable, because the organization is as much consensus as it is ukase. Perhaps herein lies the problem, and any structural change must also include charter amendment.

Part of the issue is "presence", and the need to step up to responsibility and charter. Looking at Chapter VII of the UN Charter, titled "Action With Respect to Threats to Peace, Breaches of the Peace, and Acts of Aggression", Article 41 states that .."the Security Council may decide what measures not involving the use of armed force are to be employed..., and to call on the Members to apply such measures." Article 42 states that "Should the Security Council consider that measures provided for in Article 41 would be inadequate or have proved to be inadequate, it may take such action by air, sea, or land forces as may be necessary...".

When the text and authority of these articles are reviewed, they are well intended, but are not free from political manipulation. First, the steps start with decision to apply peaceful measures, but only after the general membership agrees to apply them. Secondly, if these prove to be inadequate, (and that takes time to prove), only then can military action be considered. Further, subsequent articles of the charter discuss that member nations will then consider special agreements in support of any actions (such as availability of physical armed forces, medicine, providing advisors..). These special agreements can be a long time in the making, and certainly will relate to the special interests of the agreeing nations.

In short, although the ideas are right, the power is not vested in the organization to respond in a timely and appropriate manner.

What I really see as the implemented solution is the furtherance of RESPECT using Volitional Science as a way of socially dealing with people; and of Capitalism, as a way of economically interacting.

So once again, looking at the methodologies and adapting the United Nations into an organization capable of handling the programs, here is a suggested structure and concept of operations. Additionally, here is the combined planning and program implementation.

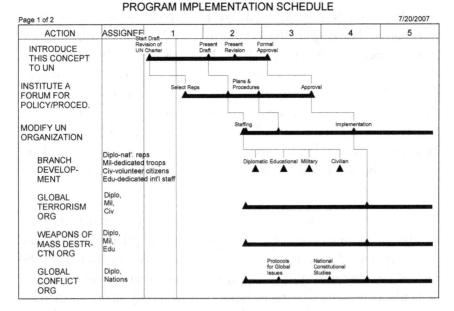

UNITED NATIONS RESTRUCTURE AND ACTION PLAN
"UN"
PROGRAM IMPLEMENTATION SCHEDULE

UNITED NATIONS RESTRUCTURE AND ACTION PLAN
"UN"
PROGRAM IMPLEMENTATION SCHEDULE

7/20/2007

ACTION	ASSIGNEE	1	2	3	4	5
WORLD ECONOMY ORG						
WORLDLEVEL EDUCATION ORG						
ANTI-DRUGS ORG						
ENVIRONMEN T						
PREGNANCY, OLD AGE, DEATH						

The combined programming for Illegal Immigration, Natural Disasters, Birth/Death/Old Age, and Drug Enforcement, relating to jurisdiction within the United States, is presented below.

UNITED STATES-THREE PROGRAMS
ILLIMM, NATDIS, DRUGS
PROGRAM IMPLEMENTATION SCHEDULE

Page 1 of 1   8/30/2006

ACTION	ASSIGNEE	1	2	3	4	5
PLAN, AREAS OF RESPONSIBILITY	INS, OHS DEA	Select Members — Initial Charter	Consideration to modify existing charters to reflect Mission Statement			
LEGISLATION, CHARTER, PLANS	Committee, Congress		Expert Memebership — Charter Approval — Plan Approval			Approved modifications, creation of charter, plans approved
IMPLEMENTATION	INS, OHS, DEA,BDO	Establish Manpower Reqts — Assignments		Active		
National Level	INS, OHS, DEA, BDO		Formation Specialized Groups — Active			
State Level	ImServ DEAEmPrep B/D/O		Define Specialty Groups — Form Groups — Active 12/18			
OVERSIGHT	Committees		Charter Definition — Active			

Appendix--Volitional Science

One of the most important topics that must be included in this manuscript is a discussion of the concept of "Volitional Science". I present it within this document because I feel that it has extremely powerful applicability towards solutions to the issues, as witnessed by its appearance in almost every section and within every subject. Notice that it stands out by frequency of occurrence, as opposed to being touted as the save-all. Of course I realize that I'm the guy creating this frequency of reference, but I find myself seeing it as a really revolutionary aspect of "World" thinking.

First some background: Volitional Science IS the interactions of man using rules that recognize respect of property, (and ideas are property,) respect of interfaces, respect of individuals. I will start out by giving the utmost credit, appreciation, and understanding of the subject to its creator, Andrew J. Galambos. This teacher was by initial training, an astrophysicist who rather early in his life concluded that the relationships of man were postured such that politics and the political mind could result in the destruction of the human race. Additionally, although man had progressed into the industrial era and was mastering the scientific, and man was moving towards understanding of the medical, that the subject of personnel interaction between men, between groups, and amongst nations was still in a political mode that did not bode well for man's future. This gave birth to his concepts of property being applied to relationships, in a way that revolutionizes the way men view each other. The nature of the mind-set that would result, he called "Volitional Science", which were presented in an amazing series of lectures, and which are at this time available in his book Sic Itur Ad Astra .

I cannot overemphasize the impact Galambos' work and teachings have had on my life and my way of thinking. You might say "I am the weirdo I am" as a result of his lectures and material. And I must give credit to his lectures and the notes I took as being the source of much of my thoughts below, of course synthesized and modified by my own life experiences since the time of my absorbing his ideas.

Some Definitions To Get It All Going

Volitional Science starts by defining property as a volitional being's life and all non-procreative derivatives thereof; (thus being anything at all)- that means physically, mentally, ideologically, whether part of you, or external-a creation of individual action. This is the breakthrough- it defines intellectual property as your innovations, your actions, beliefs, and intellectuality- orders of magnitude more encompassing than what a patent can provide, than what a dollar can buy. By the way, if you missed it, your word is your property as well.

Once you get those definitions firmly in mind, then the antithesis is seen as slavery, the control of or seizing of another's property without his consent. A thief enslaves by causing you to give him your service... i.e....property, even if he shares what he steals with someone else!!! Note that this has significant implications in the world of taxation, a subject to be covered at another time. And coercion becomes the attempted and intentional interference with another's property. Note how this has significant implication relative to terrorism.

These definitions begin the clarification of "right" actions. But, you ask, how do you know what is right? After all, you can now say that all disputes are over property, and then comes the question as to what is a standard for rightness in judging these disputes. First of all, how about that rightness is something independent of the observer; and has as a basis both truth (observability and repeatability) and validity (following the rules of logic). Right then becomes the "rational", having true premises, a valid thought process, and valid conclusions.

With rightness comes a basis for judgment, and morality. So many times we look at the logic of a thing, and see it as clearly a winner if only we can overlook some of the miniscule fine points as to whom it affects. So first lets look at what is "good". It's actually a phenomenon of and by choice, so it's a relative value, quite subjective. Add to that the fact that if it pleases at least one person and does not involve coercion upon another, <u>then</u> it jumps from relative to absolute. Morality is the totality of all absolute good, it is moral if it does not conflict with the property of another.

The Key Question, The Universal Can Opener, Is "Whose Property Is It?"

The concepts of all of man's societies will be consistent with the nature of man, existing so that individuals can exchange property. Society is a construct designed to allow satisfaction of the goal of all human existence- happiness (a relative term)- all volitional beings live to pursue happiness. All concepts of happiness pursued through moral action are equally valid. <u>Any increase in happiness derived through moral action can be called profit.</u> Profit is not the result of a loss to someone else- (that is plunder, and is obtained through immoral action), because one man's need does not represent a rightful demand on another. Based on these definitions, there needs to be a bridge of recognition that profit-seeking mechanisms are superior to other alternatives. When we talk about profit, remember that any company, organization, or gathering, is in business to make one, but due to competition, all these companies are at the mercy of the consumer. And the consumer has freedom: to choose, to spend, to occupy his time, the complete control of his own property. That closes the loop, because choice and freedom are the societal conditions through which there is 100% control of your own property.

A major mantra of Volitional Science:

THERE IS NO SUCH THING AS A SMALL INTERFERENCE WITH PROPERTY.

The science of volition deals with the totality of the exchange of property. Capitalism is one societal structure whose mechanism is capable of protecting all forms of private property completely. Carrying it further, world government, the ultimate in societal structure, would embrace the capability of integrating overall property protection. All disputes are about property, and if we build a mechanism that both minimizes disputes and handles those that remain, we can eliminate acts of coercion.

Coercion has two faces: force (the tribal chief), and fraud (the witch doctor). Even in a democracy, both majority and also minority rule are controlling. Only in an economic democracy of the market place where the best product occurs at the lowest price, where profit is the moral increase in happiness, and failure is defined as no profit (don't forget, profit could mean increase in happiness, not just financial success), can we get to true choice. This goes beyond simply the buying and selling of goods, it involves ideas and systems as well.

Two big concepts form the basis of society-the first is the market concept- produce or be replaced. The second is the government concept- protection of property, a service with voluntary subscription for protection.

Think about it, anyone can be elected to lead society if these two concepts are maintained because the market concept will assure the correct (governmental) staffing, and if the elected lead does not perform, he/she is just another "staffer" and will be so treated. This is different than the political concept-"there ought to be a law"- i.e.... the use of the gun and coercion.

So with these few inputs, the concept of Volitional Science evolves into a major human interactive dialogue. Key is the stimulation of curiosity, an essential in teaching. Note that no one said training, the term is TEACHING. Training is not education, and agreement is not comprehension. Today's school system wants obedience-the goal of a student in the educational system should again be profit, in this case the acquisition of knowledge.

All of these definitions are snippets that begin to corral the concepts of Volitional Science. This is true education, starting out with a good set of definitions, one which, when accepted, lays the foundation for thorough and rigorous examination of the civilized world as it exists today.

Now To Get It All Going

Well, the above is a really quick and dirty overview of Volitional Science epistemology. Now the application and correlations to the various problems I have discussed. Start out with a new perspective. As soon as any and all property is viewed as belonging to someone, and, that respect for property is a proper way to conduct one's business, then everything falls into place. When we recognize that destruction is an immoral act, and that the fight for ideas needs to happen on an intellectual level (at least at first in this our imperfect world), and that rational behavior is a right and conscionable way of conducting oneself, we have moved through what can be called the "zero to one transition". That means that we move from nothing to something, before this event there was no baseline, no way for things to really move forward and work; and after the event, the dialogue to create more becomes a possibility. But this will not be easy, because education will require the breaking down and correction of the years of wrong learning; in effect, a de-programming of some very powerful but immoral thought processes. And you can bet that when I say this, it is with the recognition of Volitional Science as a baseline. That is how you can differentiate between that which is right and that which is not, and the definitions are really pretty exacting, and repetitive, and rock-solid.

That is why education becomes a lynchpin, and right education is the only way for mankind to rise to its level of capability. I believe that the methods of education involve significant repetition, first to get the idea across, second to get the idea thoroughly understood, and third to get it implemented. But this is not a "1-2-3" process, it is years of exploring, de-programming, rebuilding, rethinking, and practicing. And along the way, there have to be many dropouts, because the education is voluntary, and it is not for everyone's temperament and capabilities. This is where care must be taken in the structuring of the programs, because this must never become elitist, it absolutely belongs in the hearts and minds of each and every man, woman, and child.

Do you remember Aldous Huxley's "Island", in which the entire population, partially but not absolutely secluded, was exposed to and accepted an open, loving, and logical societal set of mores, and one which existed and functioned well for many years, but was invaded, overrun, and destroyed by non-societal persons with a dedication to the mundane and crass? Well, if you either read it or remember it, you can understand why it is important that everyone embrace a right philosophy and attitude. No sense in starting something that a terrorist mentality can tear down strictly by the threat of destruction. That is why the principles of "Volitional Science" appear in so many sections of this book, because in truth these concepts must permeate existence in order to produce a way for us all to get along.

There certainly is an alternative, and that is that the technological advances would allow the isolation of those who do not embrace the philosophy. This is not to be considered as a dun, it is in fact a very logical possibility, in that if areas can be adequately isolated, then isolation would work. Come back to that at another point in time.

Return To Some Basics

Take a look at Ayn Rand's writings, some of which include "The Fountainhead", "Atlas Shrugged", "The Virtue of Selfishness", "Capitalism", oh, keep on going. She offers extremely intellectual and well-presented material that is powerful in that it lays an amazingly strong foundation for the "Volitional Science" package. This is not by chance, because Galambos' material is a next step parallel of Rand's ideas. As I re-read Ayn Rand, I felt the strongest confirmations of my own ideals and felt the strongest and deepest feelings that these ideas offer priceless guidance towards the development of a truly rational and thoroughly workable society of man.

Certain "Inalienable" Goodies

Saw a list on the internet, basically and interestingly, an in-your-face version of parts of Volitional Science, which laid out a set of standards. Because the list was publicly available on the internet with an offer to share it with others, I feel that it I can paraphrase some of the items and use them in this section, because they so clearly lay out a mind-set.

- "You do not have a right to wealth. Get it legally if you can, but no guarantee.

- You do not have the right not to be offended. In a society based on freedom, that means everyone has the freedom-not just you.

- You do not have the right to be free from harm. If you fall off a ladder, be more careful, don't look to sue the ladder maker.

- You have no right to free food, housing, or health care. Charity is fine if someone offers it, but you cannot take from anyone against their will.

- You have no right to physically harm another.

- You have no right to the possessions of others.

- You have no right to a job. If you have a tradable commodity, it is yours to use as you can negotiate.

- You have no right to happiness, only the right to pursue it."

Printed in the United States
by Baker & Taylor Publisher Services